ALGEBRA
Word Problems

BOOK 2 – ALGEBRA I and II

SERIES TITLES

Algebra Word Problems

Book 1 ▪ Book 2

Written by Anita Harnadek

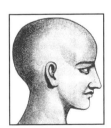

© 2001, 1988
THE CRITICAL THINKING CO.™
www.CriticalThinking.com
Phone: 800-458-4849 • Fax: 831-393-3277
P.O. Box 1610 • Seaside • CA 93955-1610
ISBN 978-0-89455-800-9

Mixed Sources
Product group from well-managed
forests and other controlled sources
www.fsc.org Cert no. SW-COC-002283
© 1996 Forest Stewardship Council
FSC

TABLE OF CONTENTS

MISCELLANEOUS 1

1. To use a lever, you need something (between its two ends) to prop it against. That something is called a fulcrum.

    Formula: (the weight you apply to your end) x (your distance from the fulcrum) = (the weight you can move at the other end) x (its distance from the fulcrum)

    Now suppose you have a four-foot crowbar and want to move a 300-pound rock.

    a–c. What is the greatest distance from the rock the fulcrum can be placed if you are able to apply weight of

    a. 50 pounds?

    b. 100 pounds?

    c. 150 pounds?

d-g.   About how much weight must you apply if the distance between the rock and the fulcrum is

d.   4 inches?

e.   9 inches?

f.   1 foot?

g.   2 feet?

2.   There are 357 calories in two slices of bread and three eggs. There are 217 calories in one slice of bread and two eggs. How many calories are in

a.   a slice of bread?

b.   an egg?

3. A jeweler bought five necklaces and three bracelets for a total of $1,000. The bracelets each cost $6 less than a necklace. If each necklace was the same price and each bracelet was the same price, then what was the cost of

   a. each bracelet?

   b. each necklace?

4. Camilla spent $3.63 on a ball for her nephew and two dolls' dresses for her niece. If she had bought two balls and one doll's dress, she would have spent $3.09. How much was a

   a. ball?

   b. doll's dress?

5. A small container of popcorn sells for 25¢, and a large container of popcorn sells for 45¢. How many of each size were sold if a total of

   a. 165 containers were sold for $54.25?

    b.   200 containers were sold for $74?

    c.   *c* containers were sold for $*d*?

6. Plain popcorn sells for 25¢, and buttered popcorn sells for 40¢. How many of each were sold if the total collected for

    a.   100 sales was $31?

    b.   100 sales was $37?

    c.   *s* sales was $*d*?

7. A spaceship was *m* miles downrange *s* seconds after liftoff. Thirty seconds later the ship was (*m* + 50) miles downrange. What was the ship's average speed in miles per hour during that thirty seconds?

8. A clothier sold ninety suits, one-third at 40% off their usual price and two-thirds at 20% off their usual price. (The two sets of suits had different prices.) If his total sales for the suits were $4,890 and his usual price was $6,750, then how much

    a. would have been the sales for the suits sold at 40% off if they had been sold at their usual price?

    b. would have been the sales for the suits sold at 20% off if they had been sold at their usual price?

    c. were the sales for the suits sold at 40% off?

    d. were the sales for the suits sold at 20% off?

    e. was the average price the clothier got for the suits sold at 40% off?

    f. was the average price the clothier got for the suits sold at 20% off?

g.   was the average usual price of the suits sold at 40% off?

h.   was the average usual price of the suits sold at 20% off?

9. One leg of an isosceles triangle is 5 inches longer than its base. Its perimeter is 16 inches.

a.   How long is each side of the triangle?

b.   What is the triangle's area? (Hint: Use Hero's formula for the area of a triangle, or use the Pythagorean Theorem to find the length of the triangle's altitude.)

10. A florist sold five dozen roses and three dozen gladiolas for a total of $105. If three dozen roses and five dozen gladiolas would have sold for $87, what was the price of each kind of flower?

11. The difference between the squares of two consecutive integers is 133. What are the integers?

12. The average score for a class on a test was 80. If five of the students had each scored ten more points on the test, the average score would have been 82. How many students were in the class?

13. Mr. Patrick is a salesman who receives a commission of 10% on sales of A and 4% on sales of B. His total commissions last week were $300. His sales of A were $500 less than his sales of B.

    a.   How much were his sales of A?   of B?

    b.   How much were his commissions on sales of A?   of B?

14. Ms. Lowry works on the same commission as Mr. Patrick. Her total commissions last week were also $300. Her sales of A were 20% more than her sales of B.

    a.   How much were her sales of A?   of B?

    b.   How much were her commissions on sales of A?   of B?

15. Five students each scored 100 on a test. The class average was 88. If there were 20 students in the class, what was the average score of the other fifteen students?

16. What two numbers have a product of 324 and a quotient of 4?

17. For the high school homecoming game, chrysanthemums were sold for 50¢ each or three for $1.00. How many were sold at each price if a total of

    a. 320 were sold for $140?

    b. 310 were sold for $120?

    c. t were sold for $$s$?

18. A dozen oranges costs one and a half times as much as a carton of milk. If a dozen oranges and two cartons of milk cost $2.31, how much is

    a. a dozen oranges?

    b. a carton of milk?

19. Jackson can do a job alone in four days. It takes three days for the job when Jackson and Corwin work together on it. How long does it take Corwin to do the job alone?

20. What two numbers have a product of 252 and a difference of 4?

21. Three years ago Jeff was three times as old as Mary was and half as old as Lara was. Three years from now Jeff will be twice as old as Mary will be.

    a. How old is Jeff?

    b. How old is Mary?

    c. How old is Lara?

    d. What fraction of Lara's age will Jeff be in three years?

22. Black pencils sell at two for 15¢, and red pencils sell at 10¢ each. How many of each kind were sold if a total of

    a. 25 were sold for $2.00?

    b. 90 were sold for $7.75?

    c. *t* were sold for $*s*?

23. Two loans totaling $10,000 were taken out, one at 10% simple interest and the other at 12% simple interest. If the interest for six months came to $560, how much was each loan?

24. The members of a computer club each contributed an equal amount to buy a printer. If there had been three more members, each member would have contributed $10 less. If there had been two fewer members, each member would have contributed $10 more.

     a.   How many members were in the club?

     b.   How much did each one contribute?

     c.   What was the total collected in contributions from the members?

25. The sum of three times one number and seven times another is 62. The difference between the numbers is 4. What are the numbers?

26. A florist sold some African violets and some azaleas for a total of $88.00. How many of each were sold if each African violet was $2.75, if each azalea was $6.00, and if there were three fewer African violets than azaleas sold?

27. 300 tickets to a concert were sold. Of these, 35 were sold at a 20% discount. The total sales came to $512.75. What was the undiscounted price of a ticket?

28. Jeans were on sale for $12 a pair, and shirts for $4.50 each. If Laurie bought a total of ten shirts and pairs of jeans for $67.50, how many of each did she buy?

29. The tens' digit of a two-digit number is two less than the units' digit. The difference between the squares of the digits is 32. What is the number?

30. If the total of Keith's and his brother's ages is multiplied by fifteen and then divided by the area of the room they share (the room is nine feet by twelve feet) and then multiplied by three square feet, the result is the age of Keith's brother, who is four years younger than Keith. How old is

   a. Keith's brother?

   b. Keith?

31. Light fudge selling for $5.00 a pound is to be mixed with dark fudge selling for $4.00 a pound. How much of each is to be used if

    a.   the total is eight pounds selling for $4.75 a pound?

    b.   the total is ten pounds selling for $4.25 a pound?

32. Ms. Gorley paid $37.80 for terry cloth to make a dozen bath towels and a dozen washcloths. If she had bought only enough to make half as many bath towels and twice as many washcloths, the terry cloth would have cost $12.60 less.

    a-b.   What was Ms. Gorley's unit cost of the

    a.   bath towels?

    b.   washcloths?

c–d. How much did she pay for the terry cloth for the

c. bath towels?

d. washcloths?

33. The sum of a number and its square is 72. What is the number?

34. The intensity of the light (the illuminance) falling on a surface varies inversely with the square of the distance between the surface and the light source.

a–c. Suppose the illuminance of a surface one foot from a light source is 144 foot-candles. What is the illuminance of a surface that is

a. two feet from the light source?

b. six feet from the light source?

c. twelve feet from the light source?

d–f. Suppose the illuminance of a surface four feet from a light source is 144 foot-candles. What is the illuminance of a surface that is

d. one foot from the light source?

e. six inches from the light source?

f. three inches from the light source?

35. The quotient of two numbers is 2. Twelve times the smaller minus two times the larger is 20. What are the numbers?

36. A beauty operator took care of twenty-seven customers one day. He gave permanents to some, and he gave shampoos and hair sets to the others. A permanent costs $35. A shampoo and set costs $7.50. The total charged for his services was $340. How many customers got

a. permanents?

b. shampoos and sets?

37. The product of a number and five more than that number is 500. What are the numbers?

38. The product of a number and seven less than that number is 98. What are the numbers?

39. The sum of the digits of a two-digit number is 14, and the product is 48. What is the number?

40. The sum of two numbers is 10, and the sum of their squares is 58. What are the numbers?

41. You have a sturdy pole eight feet long to use as a lever, and you have appropriate fulcrums for the jobs you need to do.

   a-b.   What is the greatest distance the fulcrum can be placed from the object to be lifted if you can apply 100 pounds of weight to one end and want to lift

   a.   500 pounds of weight?

b. 1,500 pounds of weight?

c-d. What is the greatest distance the fulcrum can be placed from the object to be lifted if you can apply 150 pounds of weight to one end and want to lift

c. 1,000 pounds of weight?

d. 2,000 pounds of weight?

e-g. Suppose you want to lift a weight of 500 pounds. How much weight must you apply to the end of the pole if the fulcrum is

e. 4 feet away from you?

f. 5 feet away from you?

g. 7 feet away from you?

h–k. Suppose the fulcrum is two feet from the object to be lifted. How much weight must you apply if the object weighs

  h. 100 pounds?

  i. 250 pounds?

  j. 500 pounds?

  k. 1,000 pounds?

l–o. What is the maximum weight that can be lifted if you can apply 125 pounds of weight and if the fulcrum is

  l. 4 feet away from you?

  m. 5 feet away from you?

n.   6 feet away from you?

o. $7\frac{1}{2}$ feet away from you?

42.   Find a number such that it and its reciprocal add up to $2\frac{16}{21}$.

43.   If all the eggs in a crate had been sold at the planned price, the profit would have been 20¢ a dozen. However, it was discovered when the crate was opened that ten dozen of the eggs had been broken, so the remaining eggs had to be sold at a profit of 24¢ a dozen in order to realize the same amount of profit on the whole crate.

a.   How many eggs were originally in the crate?

b–c.   If the cost of the crate of eggs was $45, for how much were the eggs

b.   supposed to have been sold originally?

    c.   sold after the breakage was discovered?

44. Topsoil and sand are sold by the cubic yard. The Mortezas' front yard, which is 36 feet by 45 feet, is six inches too low. They plan to fill in the bottom two inches with sand and the rest with topsoil.

    a.   How much sand do they need?

    b.   How much topsoil do they need?

45. What number is $1\frac{1}{2}$ more than its reciprocal?

46. A nursery sells packages of flower seeds at 60¢ each or 3 for $1.60. How many were sold at each price if

    a.   70 packages were sold for $38?

   b.   100 packages were sold for $55.40?

   c.   *p* packages were sold for $*d*?

47. The sum of Jan's age and Mahdi's age is eighteen years. When Jan is one year younger than twice her present age, she will be one and a half times as old as Mahdi is now. How old is each one now?

48. Find two consecutive

   a.   integers whose product is 306.

   b.   even numbers whose product is 288.

   c.   odd numbers whose product is 195.

    d.   multiples of three whose product is 180.

49. A bicyclist pedaled a mile in three minutes. The wheels of the bicycle, which are both the same size, revolved 720 times. Using $3\frac{1}{7}$ for pi, what is the diameter of the bicycle's rear wheel, including the tire, if the tire is a red and white plaid with traces of blue and yellow?

50. Christmas cards and decorations were discounted 50% after Christmas, when Mrs. Parker bought two boxes of cards and three packages of decorations for $6.00. If she had bought three boxes of cards and four packages of decorations, the price would have been $2.20 more. What was the undiscounted price of the

    a.   cards?

    b.   decorations?

51. The average score of a group taking a test was 80. If the six lowest scores, which averaged 50, were dropped, the average of the remaining scores would be 84. How many were in the test group?

52. If a zebra is worth eight zillers, and a rhinoceros is worth four ranguls, and a rangul is worth three zillers, then

    a. how many zillers is a rhinoceros worth?

    b. how many ranguls is a zebra worth?

53. If the numerator of a fraction is increased by 8 and the denominator is decreased by 5, the result is worth $\frac{5}{6}$. If, instead of those changes, the numerator is decreased by 1 and the denominator is increased by 1, the result is worth $\frac{1}{4}$. What is the original fraction?

54. Prove that the positive difference between the squares of any two consecutive whole numbers is one more than twice the smaller number.

55. Andrea earns twice as much as Bradley, who earns three times as much as Charlene, who earns one-fourth as much as Drew. If the total earned last week by all of them was $1,400, how much did each person earn?

56. A high school marching band won state honors in May but lost 50% of its members in June because of graduating seniors. In September it gained 125% of the remainder because of incoming freshmen. The following June, two-thirds of its members were lost because of graduating seniors, and the following September 150% of this new remainder was gained because of incoming freshmen, thus bringing the total number of members to six less than it had been when it won the state honors in May the year before. If no other members were gained or lost during this time, how many members did the band have

    a. at the start of the problem?

    b. at the end of the first June?

    c. at the end of the first September?

    d. at the end of the second June?

    e. at the end of the second September?

57. The product of two numbers is 135 and the difference between them is 6. What are the two numbers?

58. At a class meeting, 100 people either voted "yes" or abstained, 90 either voted "no" or abstained, and 80 either voted "yes" or "no." How many class members

a. were at the meeting?

b. voted "yes"?

c. voted "no"?

d. abstained?

59. The sum of the lengths of two sides of a triangle is 13. The sum of the lengths of one of those sides and the third side is 19. The triangle's perimeter is 24. What is the length of each side?

60. The average score of Ali, Brandon, and Clare on a test was 79. The average score of Ali and Brandon was 74. If Ali's score is subtracted from double Brandon's score, the result is three less than Clare's score. Find the score of each person.

61. A farmer sowed three-fourths of his land in wheat, two-thirds of the remainder in soybeans, and nine-tenths of the land still left in corn. He ended up with two acres that were uncultivated, and he planted alfalfa on those. How much land

    a.   did he start with?

    b.   was used for wheat?

    c.   was used for soybeans?

    d.   was used for corn?

62. The sum of the digits of a three-digit number is 13. The tens' digit is one more than the hundreds' digit. The sum of the hundreds' digit and the tens' digit is 5. What is the number?

63. The average score of three games Bernardo bowled was 158. The third score was ten better than the first and twenty-five lower than the second. What was the score of each game?

64. A room is half as high as it is wide, and half as wide as it is long. Its volume is 4,096 cubic feet. What are its dimensions?

65. The average test score of Alice, Bob, and Cary was 83. The average of Alice's and Bob's scores was 88, while the average of Bob's and Cary's scores was 82. What was

    a. Alice's score?

    b. Bob's score?

    c. Cary's score?

    d. the average of Alice's and Cary's scores?

66. The average of three numbers is 35. One of the numbers is five more than the smallest number and eight less than the largest number. What are the three numbers?

67. If the length of a rectangle increases by 3 ft, its area increases by 30 sq ft. What are the rectangle's dimensions?

68. The sum of two numbers is ten. The product of nine more than one of the numbers and three less than the other number is sixty. What are the numbers?

69. The total earned last week by Andrews, Baker, and Campbell was $1,180. Andrews earned $25 more than Campbell, who earned $30 less than Baker. How much did each person earn?

70. A cat is three years younger than a dog and two years older than a bird. Their ages total sixteen years. How old is each one?

71. The tens' digit of a two-digit number is three more than the units' digit. The sum of the squares of the digits is 65. What is the number?

72. If the product of Betty's and Norma's ages is nine times the quotient of their ages, how old are they?

73. The total cost of a bunch of green onions and three cartons of milk is twice as much as the total cost of three bunches of green onions and one carton of milk.

   a. If a carton of milk costs $1.25, what is the cost of a bunch of green onions?

   b. If a bunch of green onions costs 20¢, what is the cost of a carton of milk?

   c-d. If the total cost of four bunches of green onions and three cartons of milk is $4.56, then what is the cost of

   c. a carton of milk?

   d. a bunch of green onions?

74. Five people chipped in equal amounts to buy a rostrum for their club. If three more people had contributed, each of the eight people would have paid $3.75 less than the original five people paid.

    a. How much did each of the original five people pay?

    b. What was the cost of the rostrum?

75. The Barkers bought 42 square yards of carpeting and had it installed in their dining room and their family room for a total of $435. The family room took ten square yards more of carpeting than did the dining room, but the cost of the family room carpeting was $7.50 a square yard less than the cost of the dining room carpeting.

    a–b. How many square yards of carpeting were installed in the

        a. dining room?

        b. family room?

c–d.   What was the price per square yard of the carpeting installed in the

    c.   dining room?

    d.   family room?

e–f.   What was the total cost of the carpeting installed in the

    e.   dining room?

    f.   family room?

76.   A weight of 60 pounds is placed on one side of a seesaw to balance a weight of 80 pounds on the other side. If the 80-pound weight is moved one foot closer to the fulcrum, how should the 60-pound weight be moved in order to keep the seesaw in balance?

77. The total of Leonard's and his sister's ages is half as much as the age of his brother, who is five years older than Leonard and three times as old as Leonard's sister. How old is each person?

78. A batting average is figured by dividing the number of hits by the number of times at bat and then rounding the result to three decimal places. Jennifer's batting average is .353 for fifty-one times at bat.

    a. How many hits does she need in her next ten times at bat to raise her average to .426?

    b. If her average is raised to .383 in her next nine times at bat, how many hits does she get in those last nine times at bat?

79. The sum of the numerator and the denominator of a fraction is 77. If the numerator is increased by five and the denominator is decreased by two, the result is one and a half times as much as the original fraction. What is the original fraction?

80. Mrs. Wilson is three years younger than her husband, who is twice as old as their son Dominic. Dominic is five years older than one-fifth the sum of his parents' ages. How old is each person?

81. Circle A is shaded and lies inside Circle B. The radius of Circle B is four inches more than the radius of Circle A. What is the radius of each circle if the unshaded area is

a. 40π square inches?

b. twice as much as the shaded area?

c. 28π square inches more than the shaded area?

d. 16π square inches more than twice as much as the shaded area?

MISCELLANEOUS 2

1. A drafter who is paid by the hour earned $450 one week. If her hourly rate had been $3 more, she would have earned the same amount by working five hours less. How many hours did she work, and what was her hourly rate of pay?

2. Working together, Barbara, Sue, and Jane can do a job in ten hours, Barbara and Sue in fifteen hours, and Barbara and Jane in twelve hours. How long does it take

   a. each person to do the job working alone?

   b. Sue and Jane to do the job together?

3. A clothier paid $1,620 for suits to be sold at a $15 profit each. When he had sold all but nine of the suits, he had recovered his cost. Assuming that each suit cost the same, how many suits did he buy, and how much did he pay for each one?

4. Natalie is ten years older than she was when she was four years younger than she was when she was half as old as she is now. How old is she?

5. A driver's reaction time is the time between the moment a danger is sensed and the moment the brakes are applied. How many feet does the car travel before it begins to stop if

a–c. the driver is alert and has the usual reaction time of three-fourths of a second, and the car is traveling

    a. 55 mph?

    b. 40 mph?

    c. 30 mph?

d–f. the driver's reflexes are unusually fast, so that the reaction time is only half a second, and the car is traveling

    d. 55 mph?

    e. 35 mph?

f. 25 mph?

g. the driver's reaction time is t seconds and the car's rate of speed is r miles an hour?

6. Some travel club members chartered a plane for $60,000. If twenty more members had gone along, the cost per traveler would have been $100 less.

a. How much did each traveler pay?

b. How many club members joined in to charter the plane?

7. A farmer sold one-third of his hens on Monday. On Tuesday, he sold one-third of the hens he still owned. The same thing happened on Wednesday, Thursday, and Friday. If he ended up with sixty-four hens and had not acquired any hens since the previous Sunday, how many hens did he

a. start out with on Monday?

b. sell on each of the five days?

8. Janet agreed to work part time for a year in return for $4,800 in cash and a used car that was no longer driven by its owner. If she left after five months and received the used car and $1,475 in cash, how much was the used car worth?

9. If Anita were five years older and Carole were eight years younger, the sum of their ages would be twice Brenda's age. If three years is added to the sum of Brenda's and Carole's ages, the result is twice as much as Anita's age. The sum of their ages is fifty-four years. How old is each one?

10. The members of a diner's club were to share equally the cost of $1,100 for a special dinner. However, six of the members were unable to attend the dinner, and each remaining member had to pay $3 more.

a. How many members were in the club?

b. How much was each member originally supposed to contribute to the cost of the dinner?

11. (Hint: The answers to this problem are not whole numbers.)

    The sides of a rectangle are in the ratio of 9:7. What are its dimensions if

    a. its perimeter is 48 units?

    b. its area is $393\frac{3}{4}$ square units?

12. A 90,000-gallon water tank can be filled in two hours by opening valve A alone and in two and a half hours by opening valve B alone. It can be emptied in three hours by opening valve C alone. How long will it take to fill the tank under each of the following conditions? (If an answer is not whole hours, include hours, minutes, and seconds in your answer.)

    a. Valve B is kept closed. Valves A and C are opened.

    b. Valve C is kept closed. Valves A and B are opened.

    c. Valve A is kept closed. Valves B and C are opened.

d.   Valve *C* is kept closed. Valve *A* is opened. Twenty minutes later valve *B* is also opened.

e.   Valves *A* and *C* are opened. Twenty minutes later valve *B* is also opened.

f.   Valve *A* is opened. Twenty minutes later valves *B* and *C* are also opened.

g.   Valve *C* is kept closed. Valve *A* is opened. Valve *B* is also opened twenty minutes later and is then closed after another ten minutes.

h.   Valve *C* is kept closed. Valve *A* is opened. Twenty minutes later valve *B* is also opened. Ten minutes after that, Valve *A* is closed.

13.   When Harry is twice as old as he will be in three years, he will be five years older than Yvonne is then, and Yvonne will be three times as old as she is now. How old is each one now?

14. You are given a two-digit number. If the tens' digit is decreased by one and the units' digit is increased by one, and then if this new number is added to the given number, the result is 125. What is the given number?

15. The price of regular-sized cans of tomatoes is three for $1.00 at GREAT supermarket. In order to charge no more for the same quantity of tomatoes, what is the highest price that can be charged for a can of tomatoes that holds one and a half times as much as the regular-sized can?

16. Sally, Marie, and Danielle working together can do a job in two hours. Sally and Marie working together can do the job in four hours. Marie and Danielle working together can do the job in three hours. How long does it take

    a. each woman to do the job working alone?

    b. Sally and Danielle working together to do the job?

17. (Hint: Each part of this problem has four distinct answers.)

    The sum of twice one number and three times another is twenty more than the difference between them. What are the two numbers if

    a. one of the numbers is ten more than the other?

b.   one of the numbers is twice as much as the other?

18.   The sum of Jan's age and Casmir's age is eighteen years. When Jan is three years older than twice her present age, she will be one and a half times as old as Casmir will be a year after that. How old is each one now?

19.   A landscaper bought shrubs for $480. When he had sold all but ten at a profit of $4 each, he had recovered his cost. Assuming the shrubs all cost the same amount, how many did he buy, and how much did he pay for each one?

20.   The sum of the ages of Ruth, Selma, and Tom is one year more than three times Tom's age. The sum of Tom's and Selma's ages is two years more than three times Ruth's age. The sum of Ruth's and Tom's ages is the same as the sum of Selma's age and half of Ruth's age. How old is each one?

21.   If 1 is added to a fraction and then the result is inverted and subtracted from the fraction, the difference is $\frac{1}{15}$. What is the (original) fraction?

22. 12,000 pounds of paper were collected for a paper drive. If ten more people had helped, the average collected (for the same total) would have been forty pounds less.

    a.   How many people collected paper?

    b.   What was the average amount of paper collected?

23. A seesaw sits on a fulcrum. When the weight on one side x its distance from the fulcrum equals the weight on the other side x its distance from the fulcrum, then the seesaw balances. For example, 20 pounds x six feet (on one side) would balance 40 pounds x three feet (on the other side). The fulcrum of a ten-foot seesaw is placed four feet from one end. Nancy weighs 80 pounds. Homer weighs 120 pounds. Alfred weighs 100 pounds. Answer each question so that the seesaw is balanced.

    a.   Nancy sits at the long end. Where should Homer sit?

    b.   Alfred sits at the short end. Where should Homer sit?

    c.   Alfred sits two feet away from the long end. Where should Homer sit?

d.   Nancy sits at the short end. Alfred sits a foot in front of her. Where should Homer sit?

e.   Nancy sits at the short end. Alfred sits at the long end. Where should Homer sit?

f.   Homer sits two feet from the short end. Alfred sits a foot from the long end. Where should Nancy sit?

24.   A car averaged 20 miles a gallon of gas for city driving and 30 miles a gallon of gas for highway driving. If the average for both kinds of driving was 25 miles a gallon, and if

a.   6,000 miles were driven, how many miles were driven in the city?

on the highway?

b.   1,000 miles were driven in the city, how many miles were driven altogether?

only on the highway?

c. 1,200 miles were driven on the highway, how many miles were driven altogether?

only in the city?

25. A quantity of apples were sold for $15. If the price had been 10¢ a pound more, then $12\frac{1}{2}$ pounds fewer could have been sold for the same amount of money.

a. What was the quantity of apples sold?

b. What was the selling price (per pound) of the apples?

26. The value of a two-digit number is one and three-fourths times as much as the number whose digits are the reverse of the given number. What is the given number?

27. The sides of a parallelogram are 15 cm and 8 cm long, and the area of the parallelogram is 90 square cm. An altitude is dropped from a vertex to the longer side.

    a. How long is the altitude?

    b. The altitude divides the side to which it is dropped into two segments. How long is each segment? (Hint: These answers are irrational.)

28. A fruit vendor paid $50 for some oranges. If the price per dozen had been 10¢ less, he could have bought one dozen more oranges for a total of 60¢ less. How many dozen oranges did he buy, and what was the price (per dozen) he paid?

29. Machine *A* can turn out 45 bolts an hour. Machine *B* can turn out 30 bolts an hour. How many minutes will it take both machines (working at the same time) to turn out

    a. 15 bolts?

    b. 50 bolts?

    c. 90 bolts?

30. Lorna earned $99 last week. If her hourly rate had been 90¢ less, she would have had to work an additional $5\frac{1}{2}$ hours to earn the same pay. What was her hourly rate of pay, and how many hours did she work?

31. Paul works 20% slower than Marko. So Marko works _____% (fill in the blank) faster than Paul.

32. If Ezekiel's age is doubled and Thelma's age is divided by three, and if the two results are added, the answer is the mean average of their ages. If Thelma's age is doubled and Ezekiel's age is divided by three, and if the two results are added, the answer is five years less than twice the sum of their ages. How old is each one?

33. When Abe, Ben, and Carl all work together, they can do a job in ten hours. If Abe works for four hours and then Carl works for nine hours, half the job is done. If Abe works for three hours and then Carl works for eleven hours, one-third of the job is done. How long does it take each person working alone to do the job?

34. A high school history class that was open only to juniors and seniors contained two-thirds as many seniors as juniors, four fewer males than females, and two more senior males than senior females. If there were a total of thirty students in the class, how many were

    a. juniors?

    b. seniors?

    c. females?

    d. males?

    e. senior females?

    f. senior males?

g. junior females?

h. junior males?

35. Prove that the sum of a positive real number and its reciprocal is at least two.

36. The sides of Lanham's six-foot-wide front window line up exactly with two birch trees directly across the street. A maple tree grows sixty feet down the street from the first birch tree. A car came whizzing down the street at 45 mph on a clear day. Lanham, who watched the car through that window from the time the car passed the maple tree until it passed the second birch tree, said he could recognize both the driver and the front seat passenger if he saw them again, although both were previously unknown to him. If the street is forty feet from the window, and if neither person in the car had an outstanding appearance, would you tend to believe Lanham's identification if he appeared as an eyewitness and you were on the jury? How come? (You may assume that Lanham has good eyesight and is an honest man.)

37. An organization collected dues from each of its members. The total collected was $1,100. If there had been twelve fewer members, each member would have paid $1.50 more in order for the organization to collect the same total. How many members were in the organization and how much did each member pay in dues?

38. The value of a fraction is $\frac{5}{6}$ more than the value of its reciprocal. What is the value of the fraction?

39. A shopper at the GREAT supermarket can buy three loaves of bread, two cartons of milk, and a dozen eggs for $5.44; or six loaves of bread, one carton of milk, and a dozen eggs for $7.12; or two loaves of bread, two cartons of milk, and three dozen eggs for $6.13. How much does GREAT supermarket charge for

    a. a loaf of bread?

    b. a carton of milk?

    c. a dozen eggs?

40. The members of a class each gave an equal amount toward the purchase of a $14.40 reference book. If the class had had six more members, each member would have contributed 12¢ less.

    a. How many students were in the class?

b.   How much did each student contribute?

41.   The sum of two numbers is 137. The difference of their square roots is 7. What are the numbers?

42.   The formula to find the sum of the *n* consecutive integers from 1 through *n* is

$S = \frac{n(n+1)}{2}$.

a–c.   What is the sum of all integers from 1 through

a.   55?

b.   100?

c.   500?

d–f.   What is *n* if the sum of the consecutive integers from 1 through *n* is

   d.   78?

   e.   300?

   f.   1,225?

g–i.   What is the sum of the consecutive integers

   g.   starting with 601 and ending with 1,000?

   h.   starting with 75 and ending with 150?

   i.   starting with 200 and ending with 500?

j–m.   The sum of _____ consecutive integers is _____. What are the integers?

j.   50 integers, sum of 11,325

k.   10 integers, sum of 50,095

l.   100 integers, sum of 14,950

m.   25 integers, sum of 350

43.   The sum of the ages of Martha and Nick is two years less than twice the age of Perry. The sum of the ages of Nick and Perry is two and a half times Martha's age. If Nick were two years older and Martha were four years younger, Nick's age would be double Martha's age. How old is each person?

44. A plumber was paid $720 one week. If she had earned $4 an hour less, she would have had to work six hours more to earn the same amount. What was her hourly rate, and how many hours did she work?

45. Squares are cut from the corners of a rectangular sheet of metal 30 inches by 50 inches. The four sides are then turned up and soldered. How large are the squares if the volume of the resulting open metal box is

   a. 2,392 cubic inches?

   b. 4,000 cubic inches?

46. A ball is dropped from a height of 60 feet. It bounces up one-third of the distance (20 feet) before falling again, whereupon it again bounces up one-third of the distance ($6\frac{2}{3}$ feet), and so on. What is the total distance it travels?

47. You are hired for a five-year job at a starting salary of $20,000 a year. In addition, you are given the choice of getting salary raises either of $400 semiannually or $1,000 annually. (Prove your answers.)

   a. Which choice will pay more?

b. How much must the semiannual raise be in order to make it approximately equal to the $1,000 annual raise?

48. Tickets for children under 12 are $1.00. Tickets for senior citizens are $1.50. All other tickets are $3.00. All tickets sold were paid for. How many tickets of each kind were sold if the total number sold was

a. two hundred twenty, and if twice as many children's tickets as $3.00 tickets were sold, and if the total collected was $355?

b. four hundred ten, and if half as many children's tickets as senior citizens' tickets were sold, and if the total collected was $880?

c. six hundred, and if the number of $3.00 tickets sold was the same as the sum of the other kinds of tickets sold, and if the total collected was $1,250?

d. four hundred five, and if five more $3.00 tickets than children's tickets were sold, and if the total collected was $715?

49. By how much would the radius, r, of a circle have to be increased in order to increase the area of the circle by nine π square units? (Hint: The answer is in terms of r.)

50. Stock B cost twice as much as stock A, but the profit on B was only three-fourths as much as on A when both were sold.

a–b. What was the cost of each kind of stock if

    a. the total cost was $3,000?

    b. the total selling price, $2,700, resulted in an average of 20% profit on the cost?

c–d. What was the selling price of each kind of stock if

    c. the total selling price, $3,840, resulted in an average of 28% profit on the cost?

    d. the total cost, $3,000, was 70% less than the total selling price?

e-g.   What was the profit on each kind of stock if

e.   the total cost was $3,000, and the total selling price was $3,700?

f.   the cost of B was $1,000, and the total selling price was $2,900?

g.   the total cost was $6,000, and the selling price of B was $8,800?

51.   Three hundred birds were in a field. Some of the birds had two heads, and some of the birds had three legs. The other birds were normal. The birds had a total of 315 heads and 690 legs. How many of each kind of bird were there if

a.   none of the two-headed birds had three legs?

b.   all of the two-headed birds had three legs?

c.   five of the two-headed birds had three legs?

d.   one-fifth of the two-headed birds had three legs?

52.   An altitude dropped from a vertex of a parallelogram to a base divides that base into segments of 3 inches and 8 inches. The area of the parallelogram is 44 square inches. How long is the side adjacent to that base?

53.   A twelve-inch candle that burns at the rate of two and a half inches an hour is lit half an hour before a ten-inch candle that burns at the rate of two inches an hour. When will both candles be the same length?

54.   Here are Nancy and Homer and Alfred again, this time on a 12-foot seesaw with the fulcrum midway between the ends. Nancy weighs 80 pounds. Homer weighs 120 pounds. Alfred weighs 100 pounds.

a.   Nancy sits at one end of the seesaw. How far from the other end should Homer sit in order to balance the seesaw?

b.   Alfred and Nancy sit on opposite sides. Alfred sits one foot closer to the fulcrum than Nancy does. How far from the fulcrum does each one sit if the seesaw is in balance?

c. Homer sits at one end and Alfred sits at the other. On whose side, and how far from the fulcrum, should Nancy sit in order to balance the seesaw?

d. Homer sits four feet from the fulcrum. Alfred sits at the other end. On whose side, and how far from the fulcrum, should Nancy sit in order to balance the seesaw?

e. Nancy sits at one end. Homer sits a foot and a half from the fulcrum on the side opposite Nancy's side. Where should Alfred sit in order to balance the seesaw?

f–g. Nancy and Alfred sit two feet apart on one side of the seesaw, and Homer sits at the opposite end. How far from the fulcrum should Nancy and Alfred sit if

f. Nancy sits in front of Alfred?

g. Alfred sits in front of Nancy?

h. A fifty-pound sandbag is put at one end of the seesaw, and Homer sits a foot in front of the sandbag. Alfred sits at the other end. Where should Nancy sit in order to balance the seesaw?

55. A tax rate schedule shows tax due at the rate of 15% of the first $2,000 of income, 18% of the next $2,000 of income, 20% of the next $2,000 of income, and 25% of the next $2,000 of income. How much is the income if the tax due is

a. $800?

b. $1,335?

c. $642?

56. Two bicyclists agreed to a race. *B* started out fifteen minutes later than *A* and finished thirty minutes earlier than *A*.

a–b. If the race was for two hundred miles, and if *A*'s average speed was twenty miles an hour,

a. what was *B*'s average speed?

b.   how far from the starting point did *B* overtake *A*?

c-d.   If *A*'s average speed was twenty miles an hour and *B*'s average speed was twenty-five miles an hour,

c.   what was the length of the course?

d.   how far from the starting point did *B* overtake *A*?

57.   One-third of the sum of Donna's and Edwin's ages is half as much as one year more than Floyd's age. Three times the difference between Floyd's and Edwin's ages is half of Donna's age. The sum of Donna's and Floyd's ages is one year less than twice Edwin's age. How old is each one if

a.   Floyd is older than Edwin?

b.   Edwin is older than Floyd?

58. Refer to problem 56 again. You may have noticed that the b and d answers were analogous. That is, the distance from the starting point at which B overtook A was one-third of the total distance of the race.

  a. Prove that this will always be true when B starts out 15 minutes later than A and finishes 30 minutes earlier than A.

  b. Prove that if B starts out a minutes after A and finishes b minutes before A, then the distance from the starting point at which B overtakes A is $\frac{a}{a+b}$ of the total distance.

59. Pam has two-thirds as many quarters as Eugene has, and she has three times as many dimes. Eugene has 75¢ less than Pam has. The sum of the money both have is $10.25.

  a. How many of each kind of coin does Eugene have?

  b. How much money does Eugene have?

  c. How many of each kind of coin does Pam have?

d. How much money does Pam have?

60. Given that the sums of two pairs of numbers are equal and that the product of one pair equals the product of the other pair, prove that each pair of numbers is the same—that is, that one number in the first pair equals one number in the second pair, and the other number in the first pair equals the other number in the second pair.

61. Duane has twice as much money as Eduardo but only half as many coins. Both boys have nickels, dimes, and quarters. Duane has a total of twenty-seven dimes and quarters. Eduardo has a total of six dimes and quarters. Duane has half as many nickels as dimes. Eduardo has ten times as many nickels as dimes.

a. How many of each kind of coin does Duane have?

b. How much money does Duane have?

c. How many of each kind of coin does Eduardo have?

d. How much money does Eduardo have?

62. Hero's formula for the area of a triangle is $A = \sqrt{s(s-a)(s-b)(s-c)}$, where a, b, and c are the lengths of the sides of the triangle and s is the semiperimeter.

    a. If the lengths of two of the sides are 4 units and 5 units, and if the area is $4\sqrt{6}$ square units, what is the length of the third side?

    b–c. If the sum of the lengths of a and b is 7 units, of b and c is 9 units, and of a and c is 8 units, then

    b. what is the length of each side?

    c. what is the area?

    d. If the sum of the lengths of a and b is 23 units, and of b and c is 32 units, and if the area is 60 square units, how long is each side? (Assume the lengths are rational units.)

63. You are given a two-digit number. If five is added to the tens' digit and two is subtracted from the units' digit, and then the new number is added to the given number, the result is 82. What is the given number?

64. At twelve o'clock the hands of a clock coincide. They will also coincide once during each hour from one o'clock up to eleven o'clock.

   a-d. Find the exact time the hands of a clock will coincide between

      a.   one o'clock and two o'clock.

      b.   two o'clock and three o'clock.

      c.   six o'clock and seven o'clock.

      d.   nine o'clock and ten o'clock.

e. Write a general formula to show the number of minutes, m, after h o'clock that the hands of a clock will coincide, given that h is a whole number from one through ten.

65. Prove: Given four nonzero numbers such that the sum of the first two equals the sum of the last two and such that the product of the first and third equals the product of the second and fourth, then the first and fourth numbers are equal, and the second and third numbers are equal.

DIOPHANTINE PROBLEMS

A Diophantine problem* has only integers for answers, but there may be more than one answer to a problem.

Ordinarily, if you were told to solve the problem $3a - 4b = 10$, there would be an infinite number of answers. ($a = 6$, $b = 2$; $a = \frac{1}{3}$, $b = -\frac{9}{4}$; $a = -14$, $b = -13$, are some of the solutions.)

But suppose you were told that the problem is a Diophantine problem. Then the only answers would be integers. And suppose you were also told that $0 \le b \le 10$. Then there would be only three answers: $a = 6$, $b = 2$; $a = 10$, $b = 5$; $a = 14$, $b = 8$.
Check these answers in the equation to make sure they work.

In this section:
- The Diophantine problems all have a finite number of answers.
- You will be shown how to write the equations so that the answers are easier to find
  If you have a hand calculator, don't be afraid to use it. It will make some of the computations much easier.
- All variables used from now on will represent whole numbers—i.e., nonnegative integers.
- All answers will be nonnegative integers.

*Diophantine problems are named after the Greek mathematician Diophantus (*c.* 250 A.D.), who specialized in such problems.

DEFINITIONS AND RULES

We say that f is a factor of n or that f divides n if n contains f a whole number of times.

> EXAMPLES: 3 is a factor of 15.
>
> 4 divides 20.
>
> 2 is not a factor of 5.
>
> 2 does not divide 5.

We say that n is divisible by f if f is a factor of n.

> EXAMPLES: 20 is divisible by 4 but not by 7.
>
> $2k + 6$ is divisible by 2 but not by 3.
>
> Every integer is divisible by 1.

We say that *f* is a factor of *n* or that *f* divides *n* if *n* contains *f* a whole number of times.

> EXAMPLES: 3 is a factor of 15.
> 4 divides 20.
> 2 is not a factor of 5.
> 2 does not divide 5.

We say that *n* is divisible by *f* if *f* is a factor of *n*.

> EXAMPLES: 20 is divisible by 4 but not by 7.
> $2k + 6$ is divisible by 2 but not by 3.
> Every integer is divisible by 1.

A prime number is a positive number > 1 whose only positive factors are itself and 1.

> EXAMPLES: 2, 3, and 17 are prime numbers.
> 6, 15, and 77 are not prime numbers.

Two numbers are mutually prime if they have no common prime factor.

> EXAMPLES: 7 and 23 are mutually prime.
> 7 and 14 are not mutually prime.
> 6 and 10 are not mutually prime.

If *f* divides *pn* and if *f* and *p* are mutually prime, then *f* divides *n*.

> EXAMPLES: (1) Suppose 3 is a factor of 7*n*.
> 3 and 7 are mutually prime, so 3 has to be a factor of *n*.
>
> (2) Suppose 15 divides 33*n*.
> 15 and 33 have a common factor of 3.

We can divide both numbers by 3 and have 5 divides 11*n*.
Since 5 and 11 are mutually prime, it has to be true that 5 is a factor of *n*.

If both sides of an equation have a common factor, then the equation can be reduced by that factor.

> EXAMPLES: If $12a = 32b$, then $3a = 8b$.
> If $21a = 15b$, then $7a = 5b$.

PROBLEMS

1. Is 1 a prime number? Why?

2. For each pair of numbers, tell if the first number is a factor of the second.
   2 and 4;   1 and 5;   4 and 12;   4 and 14;   9 and 15;   3 and $12q$;   2 and $4k + 10$.

3. For each pair of numbers in problem 2, tell whether or not the first number divides the second.

4. For each pair of numbers in problem 2, tell whether or not the second number is divisible by the first.

5. Tell whether or not each number is a prime number. If it is not, then list all of its factors. 2;   6;   15;   17;   29;   51;   65.

6. For each number, list all of its prime factors. If a prime factor appears more than once, list it each time it appears. (Example: 4 = 2 · 2.) 10; 12; 16; 18; 50; 30.

7. Tell whether or not each pair of numbers in problem 2 are mutually prime. If they are not, then tell what their greatest common factor is.

8. Reduce each equation as far as possible.

$3a = 6b$

$6c = 9d$

$44e = 8f$

$6g = 12(h + j)$

$4k = 10m - 8n$

$14p + 35 = 21q - 7$

FIRST LESSON

Suppose we want to find all solutions for the equation $6a + 9b = 21$.

Make it simpler by reducing it: $2a + 3b = 7$.

Now solve it either for a or for b, say for a: $a = \frac{7 - 3b}{2}$.

Now start substituting values for b.

   If $b = 0$, then $a = \frac{7}{2}$, not a whole number.

   If $b = 1$, then $a = 2$.

   If $b = 2$, then $a = \frac{1}{2}$, not a whole number.

   If $b = 3$ or more, then a is negative.

So the only solution is $a = 2$, $b = 1$. Check this answer in the original equation
($6a + 9b = 21$).

Try another one: $3a + 5b = 18$.

Notice that $3a$ and 18 have a common factor. If we solve for b instead of a, we can take advantage of this factor: $b = \frac{3(6 - a)}{5}$.

Since 5 (the denominator) is prime and does not divide 3, then 5 has to divide $6 - a$. The only values of a that will allow this are $a = 1$ and $a = 6$. The corresponding values of b are 3 and 0. So $(a, b) = (1, 3)$ and $(6, 0)$.

Check these in $3a + 5b = 18$.

PROBLEMS

9. Solve the equations for *a* or *b* and find all solutions.

    a. $2a + 7b = 9$

    b. $5a + 3b = 27$

    c. $5a + 2b = 35$

10. Find all solutions. (Reduce first to make it easier.)

    a. $15c + 18d = 33$

    b. $12c + 30d = 72$

    c. $10c + 15d = 75$

    d. $12c + 10d = 76$

11. Find all solutions. (Combine terms first.)

    a. $3f - 7g + 10 = 85 - 13g - 2f$

    b. $2(3f - g) - 11 = 2f - 7(g - 7)$

    c. $3(4f + 3) - 15g = 6(14 - 3f) - 27g + 15$

SECOND LESSON

Ordinarily, for two variables, we need two equations; for three variables, we need three equations; and so on. In a Diophantine problem, however, we have only one equation for two variables (as in those we worked with in the first lesson); for three variables we have at most two equations; and so on.

We'll see what we can do with two equations in three variables:

$a + b + c = 100$

$2a + 5b + c = 120$

First, we'll get rid of one of the variables. In this case, c is the easiest to get rid of. (Subtract the first equation from the second.)

$a + 4b = 20$

Now we have the kind of equation we already know how to solve.

Solving the equation $a + 4b = 20$, we get

$(a, b) = (20, 0);\ (16, 1);\ (12, 2);\ (8, 3);\ (4, 4);\ (0, 5).$

Since (from the first equation above) $a + b + c = 100$, it is a simple matter to find that

$(a, b, c) = (20, 0, 80);\ (16, 1, 83);\ (12, 2, 86);\ (8, 3, 89);\ (4, 4, 92);\ (0, 5, 95).$

Check these solutions in both of the original equations.

PROBLEMS

12.   Find all solutions.

a. $a + b + c = 100$
$a + 2b + 3c = 105$

b. $c + d + e = 50$
$3c + 2d + e = 60$

c. $2f + 3g + h = 100$
$5f + 6g + h = 109$

d.   (Reduce the first equation before starting to solve.)

$3j + 6k + 12m = 300$
$j + k + 3m = 98$

e.   (Multiply the first equation by 2 before proceeding.)

$m + p + q = 100$
$2m + 3p + 7q = 215$

f.   (Multiply the first equation by 2 and the second equation by 3.

Then subtract the new second from the new first.)

$5a + 3b + 5c = 100$
$2a + 2b + 3c = 64$

THIRD LESSON

Now that we know how to solve the equations, we'll try doing some Diophantine word problems.

Example 1: Ms. Andrews planted a flower border fifty feet long in azaleas, buttercups, and crocuses. She spent $120. If the cost per foot was $9 for azaleas, $2 for buttercups, and $3 for crocuses, how many feet of each did she plant?

The first sentence gives us this equation: $a + b + c = 50$.

The next two sentences give us this equation: $9a + 2b + 3c = 120$.

Multiply the first equation by 2: $2a + 2b + 2c = 100$.

Subtract that from the second equation and get $7a + c = 20$.

Solve for c: $c = 20 - 7a$.

For this problem, $a \neq 0$, because we are told that Ms. Andrews planted some azaleas. For $a = 1$, $c = 13$; and for $a = 2$, $c = 6$. But $a \neq 3$, for this would make c a negative number. So we have only two possibilities for

(a, c): $(1, 13)$ and $(2, 6)$.

We put these values into the first equation ($a + b + c = 50$), and we get the only two solutions for the problem: $(a, b, c) = (1, 36, 13)$; $(2, 42, 6)$.

Check these in the original equations.

Example 2: Joy bought ten toys for $10. Balls were 25¢ each, dolls were $1.50 each, and marbles were two for a penny. How many of each kind could she have bought?

She bought a total of 10 toys, so we have $b + d + m = 10$.

To eliminate decimals, convert everything to cents. (Dolls, 150¢; total, 1,000¢.)

$25b + 150d + \frac{1}{2} m = 1,000$

Eliminate the fraction, and the system will be $b + d + m = 10$

$50b + 300d + m = 2,000$

Subtract the first equation from the second:

$49b + 299d = 1,990$

Solve for b: $b = \frac{1,990 - 299d}{49}$

This is where a hand calculator comes in handy. If you have one, see if 49 divides 1,990. (It doesn't, so $d \neq 0$.) Then see if 49 divides 1,990 – (1)(299). (It doesn't, so $d \neq 1$.) Then see if 49 divides 1,990 – (2)(299). (It doesn't, so $d \neq$ 2.) Keep going, and find that $d = 6$, $b = 4$, $m = 0$ is the only solution. Check this solution in the original equations.

PROBLEMS

Find all possible solutions. Remember that only whole numbers are acceptable as answers. Check all of your solutions.

13. Julina paid a total of $50 for some model plane kits and model car kits. How many of each did she buy if she bought at least one of each and if the cost of each plane kit and each car kit was, respectively,

    a. $10 and $5?

    b. $5 and $4?

    c. $2.50 and $3?

    d. $4.50 and $4?

    e. $7 and $3?

    f. $2.50 and $6.25?

14. An appliance dealer paid a total of $650 for toasters at $10 each and broilers at $17 each. How many of each did she buy?

15. The Super Railroad collected $210 for carrying 100 passengers to one of three cities. How many passengers were carried to each city if the cost of the tickets to A, B, and C were, respectively,

    a. $2, $3, and $4?

    b. $2, $4, and $5?

    c. $2, $3, and $5?

    d. $2, $3, and $6?

    e. $2, $4, and $6?

    f. $1.50, $3.50, and $5?

    g. $1.75, $3.50, and $4?

    h. $1.50, $3.75, and $5?

16. One hundred nickels, dimes, and half-dollars totaled $6. How many of each kind of coin were there?

17. Farmer Jones bought 100 animals for $100. Only pigs, sheep, and chickens were being sold. How many of each could she have bought if the selling prices were, respectively,

      a. $5, $10, and 50¢?

      b. $4, $8, and 50¢?

      c. $7, $5, and 50¢?

      d. $6, $8, and 50¢?

      e. $5, $13, and two for $1?

      f. $2, $3, and two for $1?

18. One hundred pennies, nickels, and dimes totaled $2. How many of each kind of coin were there?

19. Regular tickets to a play are sold for $3. Tickets for senior citizens are $1.50. Tickets for children under twelve are 50¢. How many of each kind were sold if 100 tickets were sold for $100?

20. Ms. Somers bought seventy pieces of fruit for 70¢. How many of each kind could she have bought if the prices of apples, pears, and grapes were, respectively,

     a.   10¢, 14¢, and three for a penny?

     b.   7¢, 10¢, and four for a penny?

     c.   three for 20¢, 9¢, and three for a penny?

     d.   5¢, two for 15¢, and four for a penny?

     e.   3¢, 5¢, and five for a penny?

    f.   2¢, 3¢, and three for a penny?

    g.   3¢, 4¢, and three for a penny?

21.   25% of the tickets to a play were sold at a discount of 20% from the regular price. A total of $190 was collected. If the regular price was less than $11, and if both the discounted price and the regular price were whole dollars, how many tickets were sold, and what was the regular price of a ticket?

22.   Find all positive integers such that the difference between their squares is

    a.   40

    b.   21

    c.   48

    d.   108

    e.   72

f.   112

23.   A student averaged a score of 82 on one batch of tests and 90 on another batch. How many tests were there if the overall average was 85 and if the total number of tests was less than 20?

24.   One hundred nickels, dimes, and quarters totaled $6. How many of each kind of coin were there?

25.   (Note: In this problem the *c* used is not a whole number. However, you are not required to list *c* in your solution.)

   The Pythagorean Theorem for a right triangle states $a^2 + b^2 = c^2$, where *a* and *b* are the lengths of the legs, and *c* is the length of the hypotenuse. Find the lengths of *a* and *b* if c^2 is a prime number and if the area of the triangle is (in square units)

   a.   6

   b.   12

c.   35

d.   100

e.   20

f.   210

26. In how many ways can three numbers total 100 if one is twice another and none is less than 20? List the numbers.

27. A manufacturer sells bolts in lots of one hundred for $10 a lot, or individual bolts for 15¢ each. How many lots of one hundred, and how many individual bolts, were sold if the total came to

a. $25?

b. $31.50?

    c. $60?

    d. $75?

28. Some birds, some cows, and some men were in a field. How many of each were there if there were a total of

    a.   50 heads and wings, and 70 heads and legs?

    b.   134 heads, legs, and wings, and 106 legs and wings?

    c.   60 heads and wings, and 90 legs and wings?

    d.   50 legs and heads, and 32 heads and wings?

    e.   40 heads, legs, and wings, and 32 heads and legs?

29. Given a right triangle having legs of lengths a and b and hypotenuse of length c, here is the Pythagorean Theorem again: $a^2 + b^2 = c^2$.

    Find the hypotenuse and the other leg (both whole numbers this time) of all right triangles having one leg of

a. 8

b. 24

c. 11

d. 45

e. 18

30. Consider the fraction $\frac{16}{64}$, and see what happens when the 6s are canceled: $\frac{1\cancel{6}}{\cancel{6}4} = \frac{1}{4}$. It is certainly true that $\frac{16}{64} = \frac{1}{4}$. Find all fractions with two-digit numerators and denominators such that when the units' digit of the numerator is canceled with the tens' digit of the denominator (as in the example given), the resulting fraction is equivalent to the given fraction.

31. Refer to problem 30 again. This time, find all fractions with two-digit numerators and denominators such that when the tens' digit of the numerator is canceled with the units' digit of the denominator, the resulting fraction is equivalent to the given fraction. (Or aren't there any such fractions?)

32. (This is a tougher problem than the others so far. The principle is almost the same as in problems 22 and 29, but there are more possibilities to consider.) In case you've forgotten, a rhombus is an equilateral parallelogram. Its diagonals bisect each other and are perpendicular to each other, and its area is half the product of the diagonals.

Find the (integral) lengths of the diagonals and sides of all rhombuses whose area in square units is

a.   24

b.   480

c.   5,280

d.   3,360

e.   19,656

33. A pharmacist sold 25 of one prescription at its regular price and 30 of another prescription at a discount of 10% of its regular price. How much was the regular price of each kind of prescription if the discounted price was also in whole dollars, and if the total charged was

a. $391?

b. $474?

c. $1,010?

34. Andersen's, Bauer's, and Carlyle's money totaled $100. If Bauer's money had been doubled and Carlyle's money reduced by one-third, the total would have been the same. How much did each one have, if Andersen had less than $20?

35. Dawson charged $100 for cleaning 100 items of silver. How many of each kind did he clean if his charges for teaspoons, a coffeepot, and a serving tray were, respectively,

a.   three for a dollar, $4, and $5?

b.   four for a dollar, $3, and $5?

36. A, B, C, and D decided to spend $100 on a party. Because their incomes were not all the same, they decided that the amounts they contributed would be different. How much did each one contribute toward the $100 if D's share was less than $10 and if A's share was

a.   half of B's, and C's share was four times A's?

b.   half of *B*'s, and *C*'s share was three times *A*'s?

c.   half of *C*'s, and *B*'s share was two-thirds of *C*'s?

d.   double *B*'s and one-third of *C*'s?

e.   three-fourths of *B*'s and two-thirds of *C*'s?

f.   the same as *B*'s and one-third more than *C*'s?

37.   Dawson has been cleaning silver again, 100 items for $100. How many of each did he clean if his charges for teaspoons, a coffeepot, and a serving tray were, respectively,

a.   four for a dollar, $2, and $5?

b.   two for a dollar, $3, and $6?

LESSON FOUR

Another type of Diophantine problem divides a total several times and then asks the least number the total could have been.

Example 1: Three people saw a pile of apples on sale. The first bought one-third of them. The second bought one-third of the remainder. The third bought one-third of what was still left. The three buyers then agreed to share the remaining apples equally. What is the least number of apples that could have been in the pile originally, and how many apples did each buyer get?

Solution:

Put t = the total number of apples originally.

The first buyer took $\frac{1}{3}$ of t, or $\frac{1}{3}t$, leaving $\frac{2}{3}$ of t, or $\frac{2}{3}t$.

The second buyer took $\frac{1}{3}$ of $\frac{2}{3}t$, or $\frac{2}{9}t$, leaving $\frac{2}{3}$ of $\frac{2}{3}t$, or $\frac{4}{9}t$.

The third buyer took $\frac{1}{3}$ of $\frac{4}{9}t$, or $\frac{4}{27}t$, leaving $\frac{2}{3}$ of $\frac{4}{9}t$, or $\frac{8}{27}t$.

They shared the rest equally, each getting $\frac{1}{3}$ of $\frac{8}{27}t$, or $\frac{8}{81}t$.

The least number of apples there could have been will be the least common denominator of all the fractions. The fractions have denominators of 3, 9, 27, and 81, so the least common denominator is 81. So t = 81.

The first buyer got $\left(\frac{1}{3} + \frac{8}{81}\right)$ of 81, or 27 + 8 = 35.

The second buyer got $\left(\frac{2}{9} + \frac{8}{81}\right)$ of 81 = 18 + 8 = 26.

The third buyer got $\left(\frac{4}{27} + \frac{8}{81}\right)$ of 81 = 12 + 8 = 20.

Checking, we have 35 + 26 + 20 = 81.

Example 2: This is the same as Example 1 above, except that someone else came along and bought one apple just before the pile was divided each time. How many apples were in the original pile, and how many apples did each of the three main buyers, B_1, B_2, and B_3, get?

Solution:

Put t = the total number of apples originally.

Call the individual apples sold A_1, A_2, A_3, and A_4.

A_1 was sold, so B_1 got $\frac{1}{3}$ of $(t - 1)$, or $\frac{t-1}{3}$, leaving $\frac{2}{3}$ of $(t - 1)$, or $\frac{2t-2}{3}$.

A_2 was sold, leaving $\frac{2t-2}{3}$ – 1, or $\frac{2t-5}{3}$.

B_2 got $\frac{1}{3}$ of these, or $\frac{2t-5}{9}$, leaving $\frac{2}{3}$ of $\frac{2t-5}{3}$, or $\frac{4t-10}{9}$.

A_3 was sold, leaving $\frac{4t-10}{9}$ – 1, or $\frac{4t-19}{9}$.

B_3 bought $\frac{1}{3}$ of these, or $\frac{4t-19}{27}$, leaving $\frac{2}{3}$ of $\frac{4t-19}{9}$, or $\frac{8t-38}{27}$.

A_4 was sold, leaving $\frac{8t-38}{27}$ – 1, or $\frac{8t-65}{27}$.

These were shared equally, giving each of the three main buyers

$\frac{1}{3}$ of them, or $\frac{8t-65}{81}$.

To solve the problem, we have to find a t such that all of our fractions will be whole numbers. We can eliminate some of the fractions by observing that if 3^k divides the numerator, where $k > 1$, then 3^{k-1} divides the numerator. Also, if 3^k divides the numerator, then 3^k divides double the numerator.

What the above paragraph boils down to is, we can ignore all fractions except

$\frac{t-1}{3}$, $\frac{2t-5}{9}$, $\frac{4t-19}{27}$, and $\frac{8t-65}{81}$.

Starting with the numerator of the last fraction, we will try to add or subtract enough 81's to make 8 a factor of the numerator. Then, since 8 and 81 are mutually prime, 81 has to divide whatever is left. Here we go.

$8t - 65 + 81 = 8t + 16 = 8(t + 2)$

Since 81 divides $8t - 65 + 81$, we know that 81 divides $8(t + 2)$. But 81 and 8 are mutually prime, so 81 divides $t + 2$. The least t for which this is true is $t = 79$.

Looking at the other three fractions (bottom of previous page), we find that $t = 79$ makes all of these fractions whole numbers. That is,

3 divides 79 – 1;

9 divides 2(79) – 5;

27 divides 4(79) – 19.

That means we've found our answer: $t = 79$.

> [Suppose 79 had not worked in the other fractions. Then we would simply keep adding 81's to 79 until we found a number that worked for all the fractions. To see that this would have to solve the problem, consider that since 81 divides 2 + 79, 81 also has to divide $2 + 79 + 81m = 2 + (79 + 81m)$.]

Substituting 79 for t in our favorite four fractions, we get 26, 17, 11, and 7.

So B_1 got 26 + 7 = 33 apples, B_2 got 17 + 7 = 24, and B_3 got 11 + 7 = 18.

Then 33 + 24 + 18 + 4 (bought singly) = 79.

PROBLEMS

Try to borrow a hand calculator if you don't have one of your own!

38. Upon reaching an island, s survivors of a shipwreck spent the day gathering coconuts, agreeing to share the total equally. Too tired to divide them at the end of the day, they left them all in one pile and went to sleep.

Survivor #1 awoke after an hour and, not trusting his companions, decided to take his share then. There was one coconut too many for equal sharing, so he threw it away and took $\frac{1}{s}$ of the remaining pile, hiding the coconuts he took.

Shortly after he went back to sleep, survivor #2 awoke and did the same thing as survivor #1 had done. (He threw away one coconut, took $\frac{1}{s}$ of the main pile, hid his own pile, and went back to sleep.)

The other ($s - 2$) survivors each repeated the process.

Everyone met the next afternoon to share the pile as agreed the day before. Again, there was one extra coconut, which they threw away, and then they shared the remaining coconuts equally. (You are given that there were some remaining coconuts to be shared at the end.)

Find the least number of coconuts that could have been in the original pile, and how many each survivor got, if there were

    a.   two survivors.

    b.   three survivors.

    c.   four survivors.

    d.   five survivors.

    e.   (EXTRA CREDIT!) s survivors, $s > 1$

        Hint: You may find this formula helpful:

$$\frac{a^{n+1} - b^{n+1}}{a - b} = a^n + a^{n-1}b + a^{n-2}b^2 + \ldots + a^2 b^{n-2} + ab^{n-1} + b^n$$

39. Five people found an uninhabited island and gathered dates, sharing them equally. A newcomer turned up each of the next five days. No one ate any dates until the end of this problem, at which point they all gorged themselves. Find the least number of dates gathered if each day (after the first)

    a.   the dates were all piled together again and then divided evenly among everyone, including the newcomer.

b. everyone who already had dates divided his number of dates by the number of people on the island, gave that many of his dates to the newcomer, and kept the rest.

c. the dates were all piled together again, but there was one date too many for equal sharing, so they tossed the extra date to a friendly parrot and then divided the rest equally among themselves. The parrot ate the date that was tossed to it.

d. the same as c, except there was an extra date the very first day, too. (The parrot got that one, too.)

e. the same thing happened as in c, but it went on for an extra day. (Five people the first day, and another person for each of the next six days.)

f. the same as a, but there was only one person to start with, and it went on until there were a total of ten people on the island.

40. You deserve an easier problem about now, so here's Dawson cleaning silver again, 100 items for $100. How many of each did he clean if his charges for teaspoons, coffeepots, and serving trays were, respectively,

   a. three for a dollar, $5, and $10?

   b. four for a dollar, $2, and $7?

41. Upon reaching an island, s shipwreck survivors gathered bananas and divided them equally. Each ate $\frac{1}{2}$ of her bananas.

   During the night, another survivor showed up and helped herself to $\frac{1}{s+1}$ of each pile.

   The second day, the (s + 1) survivors gathered the same number of bananas as on the first day, split them equally among themselves, and each woman ate $\frac{1}{2s}$ of her pile.

   The second night, another survivor [the (s + 2)th] showed up and helped herself to $\frac{1}{s+2}$ of each pile.

   The third day, the survivors gathered the same number of bananas as on the first day and split them equally among themselves, and each woman ate $\frac{1}{3s}$ of her pile.

a-e.   What is the least number of bananas that could have been gathered on the first day if there were originally

a.   two survivors?

b.   three survivors?

c.   four survivors?

d.   five survivors?

e.   (EXTRA CREDIT!) s survivors, $s \neq 0$?

        (Discuss all possible cases.)

f.   Suppose that each day when the survivors gathered the bananas, there was one banana too many to be divided equally among themselves, so they threw it to a friendly monkey, who promptly ate it. Then what are the answers to items a through e?

g. (EXTRA CREDIT) Given that $s > 1$, suppose that each time a pile was to be divided, there was one banana left over, which was thrown to the friendly monkey who promptly ate it. (There was one banana too many in the original pile, one too many when each woman was to eat $\frac{1}{s}$ of her pile, one too many when the $(s + 1)$ st survivor was to take $\frac{1}{s+1}$ of each pile, and so on.) Discuss a general solution for s survivors. (Or, if you think such a solution is not possible, explain why.)

h. (EXTRA CREDIT) Suppose the same conditions as in g above, except that no banana needed to be discarded before each woman ate that day. Discuss a general solution for s survivors. (Or, if you think such a solution is not possible, explain why.)

i. Do you really believe they ate all of those bananas?

FUN TIME

1. HOW TO MAKE YOUR FRIENDS THINK YOU'RE BRAINY

Here are some simple things you can do to make your friends (we'll call them Pat and Chris) think you're really brainy. For each trick, tell how you can find the number chosen, and prove why the trick works (but not to your friends, because you don't want them to know you're not really that smart).

a. Tell Pat to choose any number, add seven, multiply by two, add seven, and tell you the result. You will immediately tell Pat the number chosen. How? (I'll tell you how this time, but you still have to prove why it works. Take Pat's answer and subtract 21, and then take half of the result. Example: Pat chooses 5. Adding 7, multiplying by 2, and adding 7 again gives 31. You subtract 21, getting 10, and then divide by 2, getting 5.)

b. Tell Pat to choose a number, add six, triple the result, subtract the sum of six and the number chosen, and you will know the number chosen.

c. Pat chooses a number, doubles it, subtracts three, multiplies by five, adds four, and you know Pat's number.

d–f. You can make Pat go through a lot of calculations if you want to be really impressive.

d. Pat chooses a number, adds six, doubles the result, subtracts seven, takes six times that result, subtracts twenty-four, divides by three, adds forty-two, and divides by four.

e. You can make up your own number(s) to add or subtract throughout the problem so that the trick is harder to catch on to. For instance, Pat chooses a number (call it *p*), adds the number you choose (call it *y*), triples the result, subtracts *y*, multiplies the result by four, subtracts two times *p*, adds seven times *y*, divides by five, and subtracts *p*.

f. A variation is to have Pat choose two numbers, say *p* and *a*, and go through a series of calculations that also include a number you choose, say *y*. You will then make sure the calculations eliminate Pat's second choice (*a*). For example, Pat chooses *p*, doubles it, adds *a*, multiples by three, adds *y*, doubles the result, subtracts six times (*p* + *a*), and takes half of the result.

g. Will the above tricks work if Pat's number(s) are negative? Zero? Fractions? (Prove it.)

h. Tell Pat to choose a number and square it, then square the next higher number [from the one (s)he chose], then take the difference between the two squares. You will know Pat's number.

i. Pat and Chris each choose a number, one even and the other odd. Pat multiplies by two, and Chris multiplies by three. They add the results, and you know who chose the odd number and who chose the even number.

j. Will the trick in i above work if Pat multiplies by just any even number and Chris multiplies by just any odd number? (Prove it.)

k. Will the trick in i above work if Pat multiplies by three and Chris multiplies by two? (Prove it.)

l. Suppose you tell Pat and Chris each to subtract some given number, say g, from their chosen numbers before multiplying by two and three. Will the trick in i above still work? (Prove it.)

m–q. Convince Chris you're a whiz at multiplying and dividing whole numbers (but only by certain numbers). Tell why each method will give the correct result.

m. To multiply by 5: Divide by 2. If there's a decimal at the end, shove it one place to the right. If there's no decimal at the end, tack on a zero.

n. To divide by 5: Multiply by 2. Insert a decimal one place to the left from
    the end.

o. To multiply by 25: Divide by 4 (or if it's faster, divide by 2 twice). If
    there's a decimal at the end, shove it two places to the right. If there's no
    decimal, tack on two zeros.

p. To divide by 25: Multiply by 4 (or by 2 twice). Insert a decimal two places
    to the left of the end.

q. To divide by 25 if the last two digits are 00, 25, 50, or 75: Ignore the last
    two digits. Multiply by 4. Add 0, 1, 2, or 3 (for 00, 25, 50, or 75).

r. For m through p, state a simpler rule for the shortcut.

s. To multiply two two-digit numbers whose first digits are the same and whose last digits add to 10: Multiply the first digit by one more than itself. Tack on the product of the last two digits.

(Example: 62 x 68: 6 x 7 = 42. Tack on 2 x 8 = 16. The answer is 4216.)

t. To multiply two two-digit numbers whose last digits are the same and whose first digits add to 10: Multiply the first two digits. Add the last digit. Tack on the square of the last digit, using two places for it.

(Example:72 x 32: 7 x 3 = 21. Add 2. Get 23. Tack on 2^2 = 04. Get 2304.)

u. To see if a number is divisible by 4, see if the last two digits are divisible by 4.

(Example: $\frac{34}{4}$ leaves a remainder, so no number ending in 34 is divisible by 4; $\frac{36}{4}$ is a whole number, so every number ending in 36 is divisible by 4. So 4 does not divide either 2134 or 328534, but 4 divides both 2136 and 328536.)

v. To see if a number is divisible by 8, do the same thing as for 4, except use the last three digits instead of the last two digits.

2. THE HARE AND THE TORTOISE

A hare and a tortoise decided to have a five-mile race, but the tortoise was no dummy. The hare could obviously travel faster than the tortoise, so the tortoise insisted on having a head start of fifteen hours.

Since the hare could lope along at an average speed of ten miles an hour, while the tortoise could plod along only at a quarter of a mile an hour, the hare was more than happy with the conditions proposed.

The tortoise started off at noon, and the hare started off fifteen hours later. As he loped along, however, the hare started feeling guilty about taking an unfair advantage of the tortoise, so to make the race more even, the hare decided to lope for two minutes, then rest ten minutes, then lope for two minutes, and so on, until he reached the finish line.

    a.   At what time did the tortoise finish the race?

    b.   What was the hare's average speed?

    c.   At what time did the hare finish the race?

    d.   What is the moral of this story?

3. WHY DOES IT WORK?

A. Follow the steps below:

1) Choose a positive whole number.

2) Square it.

3) Choose the number that is one more than the first number you chose.

4) Square the number you chose in (3).

5) Add the results of (2) and (4).

6) Subtract one from (5).

7) Divide (6) by two.

   The result is always the product of the two numbers from (1) and (3). Why?

B. Try another one:

1) Choose a positive whole number.

2) Square it.

3) Choose the number that is two more than (1).

4) Square the result of (3).

5) Subtract (2) from (4).

6) Divide (5) by four.

   The result is always one more than the number you chose in (1). Why?

4. PROOF THAT 1 = 2

Suppose $\quad\quad\quad\quad\quad x \quad = \quad y$

Then $\quad\quad\quad\quad\quad\quad xy \quad = \quad y^2$

$\quad\quad\quad\quad\quad\quad\quad\quad xy - x^2 \quad = \quad y^2 - x^2$

Factor: $\quad\quad\quad\quad x(y - x) \quad = \quad (y - x)(y + x)$

Divide: $\quad\quad\quad\quad\quad x \quad = \quad y + x$

So (because $x = y$) $\quad\quad x \quad = \quad 2x$

So put $x = 1$: $\quad\quad\quad 1 \quad = \quad 2$

What's wrong?

5.   YOU ARE THE SAME AGE AS YOUR GRANDFATHER

Put y = your age, g = your grandfather's age, s = the sum.

Then
$$g + y = s$$

$$(g + y)(g - y) = s(g - y)$$

$$g^2 - y^2 = sg - sy$$

$$g^2 - sg = y^2 - sy$$

$$g^2 - sg + \left(\tfrac{s}{2}\right)^2 = y^2 - sy + \left(\tfrac{s}{2}\right)^2$$

$$\left(g - \tfrac{s}{2}\right)^2 = \left(y - \tfrac{s}{2}\right)^2$$

(Take square roots.)
$$g - \tfrac{s}{2} = y - \tfrac{s}{2}$$

Therefore,
$$g = y$$

Now, we know that you are not really the same age as your grandfather, so what's wrong with this "proof"?

6. START AND END WITH THE SAME NUMBER.

1) Choose any whole number.

2) Multiply by three.

3) Add fifteen.

4) Multiply by four.

5) Subtract twice the chosen number.

6) Multiply by five.

7) Add ten times the chosen number.

8) Divide by six.

9) Subtract three times the chosen number.

10) Add thirteen.

11) Divide by seven.

12) Subtract nine.

If you did everything right, you should end up with the same number you started with.

a. Why does it work? (Prove that it works.)

b. Will it still work if the chosen number is zero?

c. Will it still work if the chosen number is a fraction? If not, find a counterexample. If so, prove it.

d. Will it still work if the chosen number is irrational? If not, find a counterexample. If so, prove it.

7. MAGIC SQUARES

a	b	c
d	e	f
g	h	i

A magic square is square (3 x 3, 4 x 4, etc.) with the numbers arranged so that the rows, the columns, and both diagonals all have the same sum.

A trivial magic square is one in which the numbers are all the same. They're no fun, so it will be understood that the questions below are about nontrivial magic squares.

Two magic squares are considered to be the same square if one is a reflection, a rotation, or a rotation and a reflection of the other.

For example, given the arrangement of numbers here (which is not a magic square)

then

2	1
4	3

and

3	4
1	2

and

1	3
2	4

and

4	2
3	1

are reflections of it. The four reflections are across, respectively, a vertical axis, a horizontal axis, a diagonal axis (running through 1 and 4), and a diagonal axis (running through 2 and 3).

Rotations are obtained by rotating the square 90° or 180° either clockwise (c) or counterclockwise (cc):

3	1
4	2

(90° c)

4	3
2	1

(180° c or cc)

2	4
1	3

(90° cc)

a. Make a 3 x 3 magic square using all of the numbers 1–9. After you have made the magic square, answer these questions:

   1) What is the sum of the numbers 1–9? How many rows are there in your magic square? So what has to be the sum of each row, since all rows must have the same total?

   2) In (1) above, you found the magic sum for your magic square. List all the ways there are of making this magic sum by using the numbers 1–9 three at a time.

   3) Use what you found in (2) above to prove there is only one 3 x 3 magic square for the numbers 1–9. [Referring to the diagram at the beginning of this problem, how many times must a be used in a sum? Which numbers in your answer to (2) appeared that many times in the magic sum? Ask the same questions for b in the diagram. And so on.]

b. Can the numbers 2–10 be used to make a magic square? If so, do it. If not, why not?

c. Can the numbers 3–11 be used to make a magic square? If so, do it. If not, why not?

d–j.   Answer each question. If your answer is "yes," then prove it. If your answer is "no," then explain why. To make a 3 x 3 magic square, can we use

      d.   any nine consecutive positive numbers?

      e.   any nine consecutive <u>even</u> positive numbers?

      f.   any nine consecutive <u>odd</u> positive numbers?

      g.   any nine positive numbers that are three apart (for example, 1, 4, 7, …, 25; or 5, 8, 11, …, 29)?

      h.   any nine positive numbers that are d apart (n, $n + d$, $n + 2d$, …, $n + 8d$)?

      i.   any nine positive consecutive multiples ($1n$, $2n$, …, $9n$)?

      j.   any nine positive whole numbers?

k–p.   Suppose we don't restrict ourselves to working with positive whole numbers. Answer each question. If your answer is "yes, " then prove it. If your answer is "no, " then explain why. For a 3 x 3 magic square, can we use

k.   zero as one of the numbers?

l.   all negative numbers?

m.   some negative numbers and some positive numbers?

n.   some negative numbers, some positive, and zero?

o.   nine non-whole decimal numbers?

p.   nine fractions?

q–r. Is the magic square described possible? If so, discuss the requirements of the numbers to be used. If not, why not?

q.   A 2 x 2 square?

r.   A 3 x 3 magic <u>multiplication</u> square?

8. ALL POSITIVE UNEQUAL NUMBERS ARE EQUAL

Suppose a and b are both positive and $a > b$. Then there is some positive number c such that

$$a \quad = \quad b + c$$

Multiply both sides by $(a - b)$:

$$a(a - b) \quad = \quad (b + c)(a - b)$$

$$a^2 - ab \quad = \quad ba + ac - b^2 - bc$$

Subtract ac from both sides:

$$a^2 - ab - ac \quad = \quad ba - b^2 - bc$$

Factor both sides:

$$a(a - b - c) \quad = \quad b(a - b - c)$$

Divide both sides by $(a - b - c)$:

$$a \quad = \quad b$$

But we started with $a > b$, so we can't have $a = b$. So what's wrong with this "proof"?

9. THE SQUARE OF A NUMBER ($\neq$ 0) IS LESS THAN ZERO

Suppose b < a

Multiply by ($b - a$): $b(b - a)$ < $a(b - a)$

                                                      $b^2 - ba$ < $ba - a^2$

Subtract $ba - a^2$: $b^2 - 2ba + a^2$ < 0

So $(b - a)^2$ < 0

But this says the square of ($b - a$) is less than zero, and we know that no real number's square is less than zero. So what's wrong with this "proof"?

10. SOME INTERESTING RESULTS WITH MEASURES

The same procedure is followed for all problems here. A given problem always has the same answer. Find the answer and prove why it is the answer.

Here is the procedure you will follow:

1) Choose numbers of certain measures.

2) Reverse the numbers.

3) Subtract (2) from (1).

4) Reverse (3).

5) Add (3) and (4).

This is how the work would look if we were talking about ounces, quarts (32 oz), and gallons (4 qt):

1) Choose: 12 gal 3 qt   2 oz

2) Reverse   <u>2 gal 3 qt 12 oz</u>

3) Subtract: We have to regroup the chosen numbers so that the answers are positive. We convert 1 gallon to 4 quarts, and 1 quart to 32 ounces. Our problem will then be:

1) Choose (convert gal to qt):   11 gal 7 qt   2 oz

1) Choose (convert qt to oz):   11 gal 6 qt 34 oz

2) Reverse: <u>2 gal 3 qt 12 oz</u>

3) Subtract   9 gal 3 qt 22 oz

4) Reverse: <u>22 gal 3 qt   9 oz</u>

5) Add: 31 gal 6 qt 31 oz

Convert (qt to gal):   32 gal 2 qt 31 oz

a. Choose hours, minutes, and seconds within these limits: Seconds must be less than hours, and the difference between them (seconds and hours) must be 60 or less.

b. Choose bushels (4 pk), pecks (8 qt), and quarts within these limits: Quarts must be less than bushels, and the difference between them must be 8 or less.

c. Choose pounds (16 oz), ounces (16 dr), and drams within these limits: Drams must be less than pounds, and the difference between them must be 16 or less.

d. Choose apothecaries' pounds (12 oz), ounces (8 dr), and drams within these limits: Drams must be less than pounds, and the difference between them must be 8 or less.

e. Choose years, weeks, and days within these limits: Days must be less than years, and the difference between them must be 7 or less. (Use 52 weeks per year.)

f. Choose yards, feet, and inches within these limits: Inches must be less than yards, and the difference between them must be 12 or less.

11. CALCULATE YOUR BIRTH DATE

1) Write the number of the month of your birth. (January = 1, February = 2, and so on.)

2) Multiply by four.

3) Add seven.

4) Multiply by five.

5) Subtract twenty.

6) Multiply by five.

7) Add six.

8) Multiply by two.

9) What date within the month were you born? Add twice this number.

10) Subtract sixty-two.

11) Multiply by five.

12) Add thirty-five.

13) Multiply by six.

14) Subtract two thousand, one hundred.

15) Divide by three.

16) Multiply by five.

17) Add the last two digits of the year of your birth.

18) Subtract one thousand, eight hundred fifty.

If you used a hand calculator, the result should be a five- or six-digit number giving the date of your birth—month, day, year. Prove that it works.

12. THE RUNNING WHITE RAT

A psychologist cut a small circular hole in each end of a long box. A white rat was taught to start at one end of the box and run to the other end and stick its head through the hole there.

After the rat caught on to that, it was taught to return immediately to the first end and also stick its head through the hole there.

Each time the rat succeeded, it was rewarded with a small pellet of food, so the rat learned that it could keep going back and forth and keep getting more food.

Although the rat tends to be a little slow on the first trip each day, it goes faster on succeeding trips and has, in fact, been doing exceptionally well the past few days.

Today it is expected to take a full minute on the first trip but only half a minute on the return trip, and then a quarter of a minute to go back again, and so on, each trip taking only half the time of the preceding trip.

If all goes as expected, how long will it be before the rat has its head sticking out of both holes at the same time?

13. PROOF THAT 1 = -1

$$\sqrt{-1} = \sqrt{-1}$$

$$\sqrt{\frac{1}{-1}} = \sqrt{\frac{-1}{1}}$$

$$\sqrt{\frac{a}{b}} = \frac{\sqrt{a}}{\sqrt{b}} \quad : \quad \frac{\sqrt{1}}{\sqrt{-1}} = \frac{\sqrt{-1}}{\sqrt{1}}$$

Product of means = product of extremes: $\sqrt{1} \cdot \sqrt{1} = \sqrt{-1} \cdot \sqrt{-1}$

Then $\qquad\qquad\qquad\qquad\qquad 1 \cdot 1 \quad = \quad i \cdot i$

So $\qquad\qquad\qquad\qquad\qquad\quad 1 \quad = \quad i^2$

And so $\qquad\qquad\qquad\qquad\qquad 1 \quad = \quad -1$

But that's an outright lie. So what's wrong with the "proof"?

14. PROOF THAT 5 = 12

Consider this equation: $$\frac{2x-15}{x-5} - 7 = \frac{5x-20}{12-x}$$

Combine terms, left side: $$\frac{2x-15-7(x-5)}{x-5} = \frac{5x-20}{12-x}$$

Simplify: $$\frac{2x-15-7x+35}{x-5} = \frac{5x-20}{12-x}$$

Collect terms: $$\frac{-5x+20}{x-5} = \frac{5x-20}{12-x}$$

Multiply left side by $\frac{-1}{-1}$: $$\frac{5x-20}{5-x} = \frac{5x-20}{12-x}$$

If two equal fractions have equal numerators, then they have equal denominators, so:

$$5 - x = 12 - x$$

Add x to both sides: $$5 = 12$$

Now it's obvious that **something** is wrong with this "proof," but what is it that is wrong?

15. THE AMAZING SIX-DIGIT NUMBER

1) Choose any three-digit number.

2) Tack on the same number, making a six-digit number. (Example: If you choose 317, make it 317317.)

3) Divide the six-digit number by 7, 11, and 13 (in any order).

The result is always the three-digit number you chose.

    a.   Why is any such six-digit number divisible by 7, 11, and 13 without leaving any remainder?

    b.   Why is the final result always the number chosen?

16. THE ANSWER IS ALWAYS 1089

1) Write any three-digit number whose digits are all different, such that the first and third digits are not consecutive.

2) Reverse the digits and write down the new number.

3) Subtract the smaller number from the larger one.

4) Reverse the digits of your answer and write the new number underneath your answer.

5).   Add the new number to your answer. [Add the results of (3) and (4).]

The answer to (5) is always 1089. Why?

17. PROPERTIES OF RIGHT TRIANGLES

You are given the Pythagorean Theorem, $a^2 + b^2 = c^2$, in which a and b are the (lengths of the) legs of a right triangle and c is the (length of the) hypotenuse. All statements below refer only to right triangles whose sides all have integral lengths.

a. The length of at least one of the legs must be an even number. How come? (Hint: Assume both lengths are odd numbers and see what happens.)

b. The legs can never be the same length. Why?

c. Follow the directions:

   1)   Choose any two unequal positive numbers.

   2)   Square both numbers.

   3)   Take the product of the chosen numbers and double it.

   4)   Compute the (positive) difference between the squares in (2).

   5)   Compute the sum of the squares in (2).

The results of (3), (4), and (5) will always be integral sides of a right triangle. Why does it work?

18. MATHEMATICAL CHICKENS AND EGGS

If a chicken and a half lays an egg and a half in a day and a half, then

a. how many eggs will nine chickens lay in ten days?

b. how many eggs will *c* chickens lay in twelve days?

c. how many eggs will twelve chickens lay in *d* days?

d. how many days will it take *c* chickens to lay twelve eggs?

e. how many days will it take twelve chickens to lay *e* eggs?

f. how many chickens will it take to lay *e* eggs in twelve days?

g. how many chickens will it take to lay twelve eggs in *d* days?

Now suppose we want all answers in parts d–g to be whole numbers. Then what must be true about *c*, *d*, and *e*?

19. THE MONKEY AND THE BANANA

A rope is placed over the top of a fence, the same amount of rope on both sides of the fence. The rope weighs one-third pound per foot.

On one end of the rope hangs a monkey holding a banana, and on the other end is a weight equal in weight to the weight of the monkey.

The banana weighs two ounces per inch. The length of the rope (in feet) is equal to the age of the monkey (in years), and the weight of the monkey (in ounces) is as much as the age of the monkey's mother (in years). The combined ages of the monkey and its mother are thirty years.

The weight of the banana plus half of the weight of the monkey is one-fourth as much as the sum of the weights of the weight and the rope, where all weights are in the same units.

The monkey's mother is half as old as the monkey will be when it is three times as old as its mother was when she was half as old as the monkey will be when it is twice as old as it is now.

How long is the banana?

20. THE ABSENT-MINDED COOK (OR, WHICH BOTTLE HAS MORE?)

A cook has two bottles of liquid flavoring, each of which contains exactly the same amount as the other. One bottle contains almond, and the other contains vanilla.

Absent-mindedly, the cook measures out one teaspoonful of almond, pours it into the bottle containing the vanilla, and shakes the vanilla bottle well.

Then, realizing what has happened, the cook tries to make up for it by measuring out one teaspoonful of the mixture now in the vanilla bottle and pouring the teaspoonful of the mixture into the almond bottle.

Is there now more almond in the vanilla, or is there more vanilla in the almond?

Prove it.

21. THE ARROW NEVER GETS THERE

If someone shoots an arrow at you, it will never reach you. Before it can get there, it has to go half way, right? And before it can reach you, it has to go half of the remaining distance. And after that, it has half of the still remaining distance to go. But this could go on and on, and the arrow would still have to go half of some distance. So, since it still has to go half of whatever distance remains, it never reaches you.

What's wrong with this reasoning?

22. A DISCUSSION ABOUT AGES

Serge said he was twice as old as Juan would be if Juan were one-third as old as Donna will be when she is ten years older than Karen is now.

Karen said that it was stupid to make it sound so complicated, that all Serge had to say was that when Donna is one and two-thirds times her present age, she'll be ten years younger than the sum of Serge's and Karen's present ages.

Donna said they were both making it sound too hard, that it was easier to say that in two years Juan's age will be one-fourth the sum of all of their present ages.

Juan was disgusted, because it was simpler just to say that the sums of the boys' and girls' ages were equal.

How old is each one now?

23. ANIMALS IN A FIELD

Delia said she saw 100 birds and cows in a field and they had either 260 or 270 legs.

Stephen said he saw horses there, too, and the total of all the legs (birds, cows, and horses) was 300.

Jules said he saw only cows and horses and dogs, and the total number of legs was 200.

Karla said she could tell from what had been said how many of each kind of animal (including birds) were there.

How did she know, and how many of each kind were there?

24. DEBBY, JIM, KATE, AND SAM

Jim: "My computer system cost $500 more than Kate's quad system, and I can run faster than Kate, too."

Kate: "I don't have a quad system, and you can't run faster than I can, either."

Sam: "The sum of the cost of Kate's quad system and Jim's computer system is $900 less than the sum of the cost of my car and Debby's motorcycle, but Debby's motorcycle cost only half as much as my car."

Debby: "My motorcycle cost two-thirds as much as Sam's car, and Jim's computer system cost more than the two of them put together."

Jim: "Debby's right about the cost of my computer system, and I can run faster than Debby, too."

Kate: "You can't run faster than either one of us, and you don't even have a computer system."

Sam: "He got it last week, Kate, and he can run faster than you, too."

Debby: "Jim got his computer system two weeks ago, and it didn't cost $500 more than Kate's quad system."

Half of each statement made was true and half was false. Tell the cost of each thing and who runs faster than who. If not enough information is given to determine some of these things, explain why not.

25. A RETIREMENT NEST EGG

Allan said he decided that when he was thirty-three he would put a certain amount in the bank in a 6% savings account (interest compounded yearly) and leave it there for 32 years, so that when he turned sixty-five, he'd have a nice nest egg.

Mari said that if he'd invest it at 9% he'd end up with almost two and half times as much as he would at 6%.

Benjamin said if he could invest it at 12% he'd end up with about five and four-fifths times as much as he would at 6%.

Terry said she didn't understand all that high finance, that she didn't see how getting twice the amount of interest would make the total nearly six times as much, but she did know that if he invested his money at only 1%, he'd have $4,124.82 at the end of thirty-two years.

    a.   How much was Allan planning to put in a savings account?

  b–d.   How much will that amount be worth at the end of thirty-two years
           if it is invested at

    b. 6%?

    c. 9%?

    d. 12%?

26. A BASE SEVEN COMPUTATION

For this problem, you will use base seven numerals. So 10 = seven, 14 = eleven, 100 = seven squared = forty-nine, 222 = one hundred fourteen, etc.

Do problem sixteen using base seven numeration. What is the base seven answer?

Prove that the answer will always be the same. What is this answer written in base ten?

27. PROOF THAT A NONZERO NUMBER IS ZERO

Consider the infinite series

$$1 - \frac{1}{2} + \frac{1}{3} - \frac{1}{4} + \frac{1}{5} - \frac{1}{6} + \ldots$$

By taking the terms in pairs, we can see that the sum is not zero:

$$\left(1 - \frac{1}{2}\right) + \left(\frac{1}{3} - \frac{1}{4}\right) + \left(\frac{1}{5} - \frac{1}{6}\right) + \ldots = \frac{1}{2} + \frac{1}{12} + \frac{1}{30} + \ldots \text{ (The total is about .693.)}$$

Put S = the sum of the series.

Then $S = \left(1 + \frac{1}{3} + \frac{1}{5} + \frac{1}{7} + \ldots\right) - \left(\frac{1}{2} + \frac{1}{4} + \frac{1}{6} + \ldots\right)$

And $0 = \left(\frac{1}{2} + \frac{1}{4} + \frac{1}{6} + \ldots\right) - \left(\frac{1}{2} + \frac{1}{4} + \frac{1}{6} + \ldots\right)$

Add: $S = S + 0 = \left(1 + \frac{1}{2} + \frac{1}{3} + \frac{1}{4} + \frac{1}{5} + \frac{1}{6} + \ldots\right) - 2\left(\frac{1}{2} + \frac{1}{4} + \frac{1}{6} + \ldots\right) =$

$\left(1 + \frac{1}{2} + \frac{1}{3} + \frac{1}{4} + \ldots\right) - \left(1 + \frac{1}{2} + \frac{1}{3} + \frac{1}{4} + \ldots\right) = 0.$

Now we agreed above that $S \neq 0$ (S is about .693), and yet we've apparently proved that $S = 0$. Where did we go wrong?

ANSWERS

MISCELLANEOUS 1 (pp. 1-34)

1. Put d = the distance (in feet) of the fulcrum from the rock.

   a. $\frac{4}{7}$ ft ($6\frac{6}{7}$ inches) from the rock

   $$300d = 50(4 - d)$$

   b. 1 ft from the rock.
   $$300d = 100(4 - d)$$

   c. $1\frac{1}{3}$ ft (1 ft 4 in) from the rock.

   $$300d = 150(4 - d)$$

   d. $27\frac{1}{4}$ lb. $300(\frac{1}{3}) = w(4 - \frac{1}{3})$

   e. $69\frac{1}{4}$ lb. $300(\frac{3}{4}) = w(4 - \frac{3}{4})$

   f. 100 lb. $300(1) = w(4 - 1)$
   g. 300 lb. $300(2) = w(4 - 2)$

2. a. 63. $2b + 3e = 357$
   b. 77. $b + 2e = 217$

3. a. \$121.25. $5n + 3b = 1{,}000$
   b. \$127.25. $b = n - 6$

4. a. 85¢. $b + 2d = 3.63$
   b. \$1.39. $2b + d = 3.09$

5. a. 100 small, 65 large
   $c = 165$, $d = 54.25$

   b. 80 small, 120 large
   $c = 200$, $d = 74$

   c. $\frac{9c - 20d}{4}$ small, $\frac{5(4d - c)}{4}$ large

   $$s + g = c$$

   $$25s + 45g = 100d$$

6. a. 60 plain, 40 buttered
   $s = 100$, $d = 31$

   b. 20 plain, 80 buttered
   $s = 100$, $d = 37$

   c. $\frac{4(2s - 5d)}{3}$ plain, $\frac{5(4d - s)}{3}$ buttered

   $$p + b = s$$

   $$25p + 40b = 100d$$

7. 6,000 mph
   $D = rt$, so 50 miles $= \frac{r(30\ seconds)}{3{,}600\ seconds/hour}$

   so $r = \frac{50\ miles(3{,}600\ seconds/hour)}{30\ seconds}$

8. a-b. $.60f + .80t = 4{,}890$
   $f + t = 6{,}750$
   a. \$2,550;   b. \$4,200
   c. \$1,530. 60% of \$2,550
   d. \$3,360. 80% of \$4,200

   e. \$51. $\frac{\$1{,}530}{30}$ f. \$56. $\frac{\$3{,}360}{60}$

   g. \$85. $\frac{\$2{,}550}{30}$ h. \$70. $\frac{\$4{,}200}{60}$

9. a. 2, 7, and 7 in
   $l = b + 5$. $16 = l + 2s$

   b. $4\sqrt{3}$ sq. in. Hero's formula:

   $$A = \sqrt{8(8 - 2)(8 - 7)(8 - 7)}$$

10. \$7.50 a dozen for gladiolas. \$16.50 a dozen for roses.
    $5r + 3g = 105$; $3r + 5g = 87$

11. 66 and 67 **or** −66 and −67
    $(n + 1)^2 - n^2 = 133$
    or $n^2 - (n + 1)^2 = 133$

12. 25. $80n = t$. $82n = t + 5(10)$

13. a. \$2000; \$2,500
    $.10A + .04B = 300$; $A = B - 500$
    b. \$200; \$100. $C_A = .10(2{,}000)$;
    $C_B = .04(2{,}500)$ **or** $300 - 200$

14. a. \$2,250; \$1,875. $10A + .04B = 300$
    $A = 1.20B$
    b. \$225; \$75. $C_A = .10(2{,}250)$;
    $C_B = .04(1{,}875)$ **or** $300 - 225$

15. 84. $15a + 5(100) = 20(88)$

16. 9 and 36 **or** –9 and –36
$ab = 324; \frac{a}{b} = 4$

17. **a.** 200 @ 50¢, 120 @ 3 for $1
$t = 320, s = 140$

    b. 100 @ 50¢, 210 @ 3 for $1
$t = 310, s = 120$

    c. 2(3s - t) @ 50¢,
3(t - 2s) @ 3 for $1
$f + d = t$

        $50f + \frac{100d}{3} = 100s$

18. **a.** 99¢   **b.** 66¢
$g = \frac{3}{2}m$

    $g + 2m = 231$

19. 12 days. $\frac{1}{4} + \frac{1}{c} = \frac{1}{3}$

20. 14 and 18; –14 and –18
$ab = 252; a - b = 4$

21. **a.** 21   **b.** 9
    c. 39   **d.** $\frac{4}{7}$

  a–c. $J - 3 = 3(M - 3) = \frac{1}{2}(L - 3)$

      $J + 3 = 2(M + 3)$

    d. $\frac{21 + 3}{39 + 3}$

22. **a.** 20 black, 5 red. $t = 25, s = 2.00$

    b. 50 black, 40 red. $t - 90, s = 7.75$

    c. 4(t - 10s) black, (40s - 3t) red
$b + r = t$

      $\frac{15}{2}b + 10s = 100s$

23. $4,000 at 10%, $6,000 at 12%
$t + v = 10,000$
$.10t + .12v = 2(560)$

24. **a.** 12   **b.** $50   **c.** $600
$mc = t$
$(m + 3)(c - 10) = t$
$(m - 2)(c + 10) = t$

25. 9 and 5 **or** $3\frac{2}{5}$ and $7\frac{2}{5}$
$3a + 7b = 62$

    $a - b = 4$ or $b - a = 4$

26. 11 azaleas, 8 African violets
$2.75v + 6a = 88$
$v = a - 3$

27. $1.75
$(300 - 35)p + 35(.80p) = 512.75$

28. 7 shirts, 3 pairs of jeans. $j + s = 10$
$12j + 4.50s = 67.50$

29. 79. $t = u - 2$
$u^2 - t^2 = 32$

30. **a.** 10   **b.** 14

    $\left(\frac{15(K + B)}{(9 \times 12)\text{sqft}}\right)(3 \text{ sq ft}) = B$

    $B = K - 4$

31. **a.** 6 lb of light, 2 lb of dark
$t + d = 8$
$5t + 4d = 4.75(8)$

    b. $2\frac{1}{2}$ lb of light, $7\frac{1}{2}$ lb of dark
$t + d = 10$
$5t + 4d = 4.25(10)$

32. **a.** $2.80   **b.** 35¢
  a–b. $12b + 12w = 37.80$
$6b + 24w = 37.80 - 12.60$
    c. $33.60. 12($2.80)
    d. $4.20. 12($.35)

33. 8 **or** –9. $n^2 + n = 72$

34. $k = id^2$
  a–c. $k = 144(1)^2 = 144$
    a. 36 foot-candles. $144 = i(2)^2$

    b. 4 foot-candles. $144 = i(6)^2$

    c. 1 foot-candle. $144 = i(12)^2$

  d–f. $k = 144(4)^2 = 2,304$
    d. 2,304 foot-candles. $2,304 = i(1)^2$

    e. 9,216 foot-candles. $2,304 = i(\frac{1}{2})^2$

f. 36,864 foot-candles
$2{,}304 = i(\frac{1}{4})^2$

35. $2\frac{1}{2}$ and 5. $\frac{a}{b} = 2$. $12b - 2a = 20$

36. a. 5   **b.** 22
$p + s = 27$
$35p + 7.50s = 340$

37. 20 and 25 **or** −25 and −20
$n(n + 5) = 500$

38. 14 and 7 **or** −7 and −14
$n(n - 7) = 98$

39. 68 **or** 86. $t + u = 14$; $tu = 48$

40. 3 and 7. $a + b = 10$; $a^2 + b^2 = 58$

41. Put d = the distance (in ft) between the fulcrum and the object to be lifted.

a. $1\frac{1}{3}$ ft (1ft 4 in). $500d = 100(8 - d)$

b. $\frac{1}{2}$ ft (6 in). $1{,}500d = 100(8 - d)$

c. $1\frac{1}{23}$ ft $\left(1\ \text{ft}\frac{12}{23}\ \text{in}\right)$

$1{,}000d = 150(8 - d)$

d. $\frac{24}{43}$ft $\left(6\frac{30}{43}\ \text{in}\right)$. $2{,}000d = 150(8 - d)$

e. 500 lb. $500(8 - 4) = 4w$

f. 300 lb. $500(8 - 5) = 5w$

g. $71\frac{3}{7}$ lb. $500(8 - 7) = 7w$

h. $33\frac{1}{3}$ lb. $100(2) = 6w$

i. $83\frac{1}{3}$ lb. $250(2) = 6w$

j. $166\frac{2}{3}$ lb. $500(2) = 6w$

k. $333\frac{1}{3}$ lb. $1{,}000(2) = 6w$

l. 125 lb. $(8 - 4)w = 4(125)$

m. $208\frac{1}{3}$ lb. $(8 - 5)w = 5(125)$

n. 375 lb. $(8 - 6)w = 6(125)$

o. 1,875 lb. $(8 - 7\frac{1}{2})w = (7\frac{1}{2})(125)$

42. $\frac{3}{7}$ or $\frac{7}{3}$. $n + \frac{1}{n} = 2\frac{16}{21}$

43. a. 60 dozen. $p = 20d$; $p = 24(d - 10)$

b–c. From **a**, the total profit is $12.

b. 95¢ a dozen

$s = \frac{45 + 12}{60}$ or $s = \frac{45}{60} + .20$

c. $1.14 a dozen.
$s = \frac{45 + 12}{50}$ or $s = \frac{45}{50} + .24$

44. 1 cubic yard = 1(yard)³ = 1(3 feet)³ = 27 cubic feet, so

a. 10 cubic yards. $27y = 36(45)(\frac{1}{6})$

b. 20 cubic yards. $27y = 36(45)(\frac{1}{3})$

45. 2 or $-\frac{1}{2}$. $n = \frac{1}{n} + 1\frac{1}{2}$

46. a. 10 @ 60¢, 60 @ 3 for $1.60
$p = 70$, $d = 38$

b. 31 @ 60¢, 69 @ 3 for $1.60
$p = 100$, $d = 55.40$

c. $(15d - 8p)$ @ 60¢, $(9p - 15d)$ @ 3 for $1.60

$s + t = p$; $.60s + \frac{1.60t}{3} = d$

47. Jan is 10, Mahdi is 8. $J + M = 18$;

$2J - 1 = \frac{3}{2}M$

48. a. 17 and 18 **or** −18 and −17
$n(n + 1) = 306$

b. 16 and 18 **or** −16 and −18
$n(n + 2) = 288$

c. 13 and 15 **or** −15 and −13
$n(n + 2) = 195$
Note: Ask your students how come both **b** and **c** can use the same expression—i.e., $n(n + 2)$—and yet have one answer come out even and the other answer come out odd.

d. 12 and 15 **or** –15 and –12

$3n[3(n + 1)] = 180$.

49. 28 in. $\frac{5{,}280 \text{ feet}}{\text{mile}} \times \frac{12 \text{ inches}}{\text{foot}} = \frac{63{,}360 \text{ inches}}{\text{mile}}$

$\frac{63{,}360}{720}$ = 88 inches traveled in each revolution, or a circumference of the wheel (including the plaid tire) of 88 inches. Circumference of a circle = πd, or $(3\frac{1}{7})d$, so $(\frac{22}{7})d = 88$.

50. **a.** $1.20 a box x 2 boxes = $2.40

b. $3.20 a package x 3 packages = $9.60. We can let c, d = the undiscounted prices, in which case we double the given purchase prices, or we can let c, d = the discounted prices, in which case we double c and d (once we solve the system for c and d) to get the undiscounted prices. Here is the first way:

$2c + 3d = 2(6)$

$3c + 4d = 2(6 + 2.20)$.

51. 51. $80n = t$; $84(n – 6) = t – 6(50)$

52. **a.** 12   **b.** $2\frac{2}{3}$

$z = 8Z$

$r = 4R$

$R = 3Z$

53. $\frac{7}{23} \cdot \frac{n+8}{d-5} = \frac{5}{6}$; $\frac{n-1}{d+1} = \frac{1}{4}$

54. $(n + 1)^2 – n^2 = n^2 + 2n + 1 – n^2 = 2n + 1$ = one more than two times n.

55. Andrea, $600; Bradley, $300; Charlene, $100; Drew, $400.

$A = 2B$

$B = 3C$

$C = (\frac{1}{4})D$

$A + B + C + D = 1{,}400$

56. **a.** 96   **b.** 48

c. 108   **d.** 36   **e.** 90

Put t = the total number of band members at the start of the problem. The first June, .50t were lost, leaving .50t. That September,

1.25(.50t) were gained, making a total of 1.25(.50t) + .50t, or 1.125t. The next June, $\frac{2}{3}$(1.125t) were lost, leaving $\frac{1}{3}$(1.125t), or .375t. The last September, 1.50(.375t) were gained, making a total of 1.50(.375t) + .375t, or .9375t, which is given as t – 6. So .9375t = t – 6.

57. 15 and 9 **or** –9 and –15. $ab = 135$

$a – b = 6$

58. **a.** 135   **b.** 45

c. 35   **d.** 55. $y + a = 100$

$n + a = 90$

$y + n = 80$

59. 5, 8, and 11. $a + b = 13$

$a + c = 19$

$a + b + c = 24$

60. Ali, 70; Brandon, 78; Clare, 89

$\frac{A + B + C}{3}$ = 79

$\frac{A + B}{2}$ = 74

$2B – A = C – 3$

61. **a.** 240 acres   **b.** 180 acres

c. 40 acres   **d.** 18 acres

$w = \frac{1}{4} t$

$s = \frac{2}{3}(t – w)$

$c = \frac{9}{10}(t – w – s)$

$t = 2 + w + s + c$

62. 238. $h + t + u = 13$

$t = h + 1$

$h + t = 5$

63. 143, 178, and 153. $\frac{f + s + t}{3}$ = 158

$t = f + 10 = s – 25$

64. 16 feet wide by 32 feet long by 8 feet high. $V = lwh = 4{,}096$

$h = \frac{1}{2} w$ $w = \frac{1}{2} l$

65. **a.** 85   **b.** 91
  c. 73   **d.** 79

  a–c. $\frac{A + B + C}{3} = 83$

  $\frac{A + B}{2} = 88$

  $\frac{B + C}{2} = 82$

  d. $\frac{85 + 73}{2}$

66. 29, 34, 42. $\frac{a + b + c}{3} = 35$

  $b = a + 5 = c - 8$

67. The width is 10 ft. Not enough information is given to determine the length. $A = lw$
$A + 30 = (l + 3)w$

68. –3 and 13 **or** 1 and 9. $a + b = 10$
$(a + 9)(b - 3) = 60$

69. Andrews, $400; Baker, $405; Campbell, $375. $A + B + C = 1{,}180$
$A = C + 25$
$C = B - 30$

70. The bird is 3, the cat is 5, and the dog is 8. $C = D - 3$
$C = B + 2$
$B + C + D = 16$

71. 74. $t = u + 3$
$t^2 + u^2 = 65$

72. One is 3. Not enough information is given to determine the other's age.
$BN = \frac{9B}{N}$ or $BN = \frac{9N}{B}$

73. $g + 3m = 2(3g + m)$

  a. 25¢. $g + 3(125) = 2(3g + 125)$
  b. $1.00. $20 + 3m = 2[3(20) + m]$
  c. $1.20   **d.** 24¢
  c–d. $4g + 3m = 4.56$

74. **a.** $10. $5a = t$
  $(8a - 3.75) = t$
  b. $50. $5($10)

75. **a–b.** $d + f = 42$
  $f = d + 10$
  a. 16   **b.** 26
  c–d. $16D + 26F = 435$
  $F = D - 7.50$
  c. $15   **d.** $7.50
  e. $240. 16($15)
  f. $195. 26($7.50)

76. It should be moved $1\frac{1}{3}$ ft closer to the fulcrum. Put d = the additional distance away from the fulcrum the 60-pound weight is to be moved.

  Put s, e = the distances away from the fulcrum the 60- and 80-pound weights have already been placed.

  $60s = 80e$
  $60(s + d) = 80(e - 1)$
  (Solve for d.)

77. Leonard is 1, his sister is 2, and his brother is 6. $L + S = \frac{1}{2}B$
$B = L + 5$
$B = 3S$

78. By definition of batting average, Jennifer's number of hits so far approximates 51(.353), or 18. As we do the problem, we keep in mind that hits and at-bats must both be whole numbers.

  a. 8. $.426 = \frac{18 + h}{51 + 10}$

  b. 5. $.383 = \frac{18 + h}{51 + 9}$

79. $\frac{11}{66}$. $n + d = 77$

  $\frac{n + 5}{d - 2} = \frac{3}{2}\left(\frac{n}{d}\right)$

  Note: $\frac{70}{7}$ is also an answer, but since

  $\frac{70}{7} = 10$, a whole number, it was excluded from the answer. You can make the decision as to whether or not $\frac{70}{7}$ should be accepted as a "fraction" within the context of the problem.

80. Dominic is 22; his mother is 41; his father is 44. $M = F - 3$

$F = 2D$

$D = \frac{1}{5}(M + F) + 5$

81. $A = \pi r^2$

$A_U = A_B - A_A$

$r_B = r_A + 4$

$A_U = (r_A + 4)2\pi - r_A 2\pi$

a. A, 3in.; B, 7 in. $A_U = 40\pi$

b. A, $(2 + 2\sqrt{3})$ in.; B, $(6 + 2\sqrt{3})$ in. $A_U = 2A_A$

c. A, 2 in.; B, 6 in. **or** A, 6 in.; B, 10 in. $A_U = A_A + 28$

d. A, 4 in.; B, 8 in. $A_U = 2A_A + 16$

MISCELLANEOUS 2 (pp. 35-66)

1. 30, $15. $hr = 450$

$(h - 5)(r + 3) = 450$

2. a. 20 hours for Barbara, 30 hours for Jane, 60 hours for Sue.

$\frac{1}{B} + \frac{1}{S} + \frac{1}{J} = \frac{1}{10}$

$\frac{1}{B} + \frac{1}{S} = \frac{1}{15}$

$\frac{1}{B} + \frac{1}{J} = \frac{1}{12}$

b. 20 hours. $\frac{1}{60} + \frac{1}{30} = \frac{1}{h}$

3. 36 suits at $45 each. $np = 1,620$
$(n - 9)(p + 15) = 1,620$

4. 12 years. $N = 10 + (\frac{N}{2} - 4)$

5. a–f. Using the formula below gives us

a. $60\frac{1}{2}$. $D = \frac{22}{15}(55)(\frac{3}{4})$

b. 44. 1 hr. $D = (40)(\frac{3}{4})$

c. 33. $D = \frac{22}{15}(30)(\frac{3}{4})$

d. $40\frac{1}{3}$. $D = \frac{22}{15}(55)(\frac{1}{2})$

e. $25\frac{2}{3}$. $D = \frac{22}{15}(35)(\frac{1}{2})$

f. $18\frac{1}{3}$. $D = \frac{22}{15}(25)(\frac{1}{2})$

g. $D = \frac{22}{15}rt$

$D = rt$, so distance in feet =

$\frac{r \text{ miles}}{\text{hours}}\left(\frac{5,280 \text{ feet}}{\text{miles}}\right)\left(\frac{\text{hours}}{3,600 \text{ seconds/hour}}\right) \times$

$(t \text{ seconds}) = \frac{5,280}{3,600}rt$, where r is

in mph and t is in seconds.

Simplifying, we have $D = \frac{22}{15}rt$.

6. a. $600   **b.** 100
$mc = 60,000$
$(m + 20)(c - 100) = 60,000$

7. a. 486. On Friday, he ended up with 64 hens, which was $\frac{2}{3}$ of $\frac{2}{3}$ of $\frac{2}{3}$ of $\frac{2}{3}$ of $\frac{2}{3}$ of his hens.

So $64 = (\frac{2}{3})^5 h = \frac{32}{243}h$.

b. 162 Monday, 108 Tuesday, 72 Wednesday, 48 Thursday, 32 Friday. On Monday, he sold $\frac{1}{3}$ of 486, or 162. On each successive day, he sold $\frac{1}{3}$ of the $\frac{2}{3}$ left. But it is easier to take $\frac{2}{3}$ of the $\frac{1}{3}$ he sold the previous day.

8. $900. Her wages for a year were $4,800 + the value of the car, or

$(4,800 + c)$. She worked for 5 months, or $\frac{5}{12}$ of the year, so

$\frac{5}{12}(4,800 + c) = 1,475 + c$.

9. Anita is 19; Brenda is 17; Carole is 18. $(A + 5) + (C - 8) = 2B$
$(B + C) + 3 = 2A$
$A + B + C = 54$

10. **a.** 50   **b.** $22
$mc = 1,100$
$(m - 6)(c + 3) = 1,100$

11. **a.** $10\frac{1}{2}$ units wide by $13\frac{1}{2}$ units long

$2(l + w) = 48$

b. $17\frac{1}{2}$ units wide by $22\frac{1}{2}$ units long

$lw = 393.75$

12. The capacity of the tank can be ignored, treating the tank to be filled (or emptied) as one full job to be done, and using $\frac{1}{A}$, $\frac{1}{B}$, and $\frac{1}{C}$ in the equations. But it seems easier to proceed as follows:

A fills the tank at the rate of

$\frac{90,000}{2(60)} = 750$ gal/min

B fills the tank at the rate of

$\frac{90,000}{2.5(60)} = 600$ gal/min

C empties the tank at the rate of

$\frac{90,000}{3(60)} = 500$ gal/min

a. 6 hr. $m(750 - 500) = 90,000$

b. 1 hr 6 min 40 sec. $m(750 + 600) = 90,000$

c. 15 hr. $m(600 - 500) = 90,000$

d. 55 min $33\frac{1}{3}$ sec. $20(750) + m(750 + 600) = 90,000$

e. 1 hr 40 min. $20(750 - 500) + m(750 + 600 - 500) = 90,000$

f. 1 hr 28 min. $14\frac{2}{17}$ sec. $20(750) + m(750 + 600 - 500) = 90,000$

g. 1 hr 22 min. $20(750) + 10(750 + 600) + m(750) = 90,000$

h. 1 hr 42 min. 30 sec $20(750) = 10(750 + 600) + m(600) = 90,000$

13. Yvonne is 11; Harry is 16.
$H = Y + 5$ $Y + [2(H + 3) - H] = 3Y$

14. 67. Given $10t + u$.
$10(t - 1) + (u + 1) + 10t + u = 125$,
so $10(2t - 1) + 2u + 1 = 125$.
Then $2u + 1 = 5$ or 15.
If $2u + 1 = 5$, then $2t - 1 = 12$, a contradiction.
So $2u + 1 = 15$, and $u = 7$.
Then $125 = 10(2t - 1) + 15$,
so $110 = 20t - 10$, and $t = 6$.

15. 50¢. An understandable way to do such a problem is to use ratio and proportion:

$\frac{\text{quantity no. 1}}{\text{price no. 1}} = \frac{\text{quantity no. 2}}{\text{price no. 2}}$.

So $\frac{q}{\frac{100}{3}} = \frac{\frac{3}{2}q}{p}$, and so $p = \frac{3}{2}\left(\frac{100}{3}\right) = 50$.

16. **a.** 12 hr for Marie, 4 hr for Danielle, 6 hr for Sally.

$\frac{1}{S} + \frac{1}{M} + \frac{1}{D} = \frac{1}{2}$

$\frac{1}{S} + \frac{1}{M} = \frac{1}{4}$

$\frac{1}{M} + \frac{1}{D} = \frac{1}{3}$

$\frac{1}{6} + \frac{1}{4} = \frac{1}{h}$

b. $2\frac{2}{5}$ hr

17. $2a + 3b = 20 + (a - b)$ **or**
$2a + 3b = 20 + (b - a)$

a. 12 and 2 **or** –4 and 6 **or** 8 and –2
or 0 and 10.
$a = b + 10$ **or** $b = a + 10$

b. $6\frac{2}{3}$ and $3\frac{1}{3}$ **or** $2\frac{2}{9}$ and $4\frac{4}{9}$ **or** 5

and $2\frac{1}{2}$ **or** $2\frac{6}{7}$ and $5\frac{5}{7}$.

$a = 2b$ **or** $b = 2a$

18. Jan is 15; Casmir is 3. When Jan is
three years older than twice her
present age, she will be $2J + 3$,
which is $J + 3$ years older than she
is now. At that point, Casmir, too,
will be $J + 3$ years older than he is
now, so his age will be $C + J + 3$. So
$J + C = 18$.

$2J + 3 = \frac{3}{2}[(C + J + 3) + 1]$

19. 40 at \$12. $np = 480$
$(n - 10)(p + 4) = 480$

20. Ruth is 8; Tom is 11; Selma is 15.
$R + S + T = 3T + 1$
$S + T = 3R + 2$
$R + T = S + \frac{1}{2}R$

21. $-\frac{8}{5}$ **or** $\frac{2}{3}$

$\frac{n}{d} - \frac{1}{\frac{n}{d} + 1} = \frac{1}{15}$

22. $ap = 12{,}000$
$(a - 40)(p + 10) = 12{,}000$
a. 50   b. 240 lb

23. a. at the other end. $80(6) = 120d$

b. on the other side $3\frac{1}{3}$ ft from the

fulcrum ($2\frac{2}{3}$ ft from the end).

$100(4) = 120d$

c. on the other side $3\frac{1}{3}$ ft from the

fulcrum ($\frac{2}{3}$ ft from the end.)

$100(4) = 120d$

d. on the other side $5\frac{1}{6}$ ft from the

fulcrum (10 in. from the end).
$80(4) + 100(3) = 120d$

e. on Nancy's side $2\frac{1}{3}$ ft from the

fulcrum ($1\frac{2}{3}$ ft in front of Nancy).
$80(4) + 120d = 100(6)$

f. on Homer's side $3\frac{1}{4}$ ft from the

fulcrum ($1\frac{1}{4}$ ft behind Homer).
$120(2) + 80d = 100(5)$

24. Put c = miles driven in the city.
Put h = miles driven on the highway.
Then $\frac{c}{20} + \frac{h}{30} = \frac{c + h}{25}$

a. 2,400; 3,600. $c + h = 6{,}000$
b. 2,500; 1,500. $c = 1{,}000$
c. 2,000; 800. $h = 1{,}200$

25. $pq = 1{,}500$
$(p + 10)(q - \frac{25}{2}) = 1{,}500$
a. 50 lb   b. 30¢ a lb

26. 21, 42, 63, or 84

$10t + u = \frac{7}{4}(10u + t)$

27. a. 6 cm. $90 = 15a$

b. $2\sqrt{7}$ and $15 - 2\sqrt{7}$. Use the
Pythagorean Theorem to get the
length of the shorter segment, s.
Then the longer segment is $15 - s$.

28. 25; \$2 a doz. $dp = 50$
$(p - .10)(d + 1) = 50 - .60$

29. A's rate of work is $\frac{45}{60} = \frac{3}{4}$ bolt a

minute. B's rate is $\frac{30}{60} = \frac{1}{2}$ bolt a

minute. Then together they will

make $\frac{3}{4} + \frac{1}{2} = \frac{5}{4}$ bolts a minute.

  a. 12 min. $m(\frac{5}{4}) = 15$

  b. 40 min. $m(\frac{5}{4}) = 50$

  c. 72 min. $m(\frac{5}{4}) = 90$

30. $4.50; 22. $rh = 99$

$(r - .90)(h + 5\frac{1}{2}) = 99$

31. 25. Paul works at 80% of Marko's

rate, so $\frac{1}{P} = .80(\frac{1}{M}) = \frac{4}{5}(\frac{1}{M})$, and so

$\frac{1}{M} = (\frac{5}{4})(\frac{1}{P}) = 1.25(\frac{1}{P}) = 25\%$ more

than $\frac{1}{P}$. It is simpler here to put P,

M = Paul's and Marko's rates of
work, and then we have $P = .80M$

$= \frac{4}{5}M$, so $M = \frac{5}{4}P = 1.25P$.

32. Ezekiel is 3; Thelma is 27.

$2E + \frac{T}{3} = \frac{E + T}{2}$

$2T + \frac{E}{3} = 2(E + T) - 5$

33. Abe, 20 hr; Ben, 30 hr; Carl, 60 hr

$\frac{1}{A} + \frac{1}{B} + \frac{1}{C} = \frac{1}{10}$

$\frac{4}{A} + \frac{9}{C} = \frac{1}{2}$

$\frac{3}{A} + \frac{11}{C} = \frac{1}{3}$

34. a–b. $j + s = 30. \; s = \frac{2}{3} j$

  a. 18   **b.** 12

 c–d. $m + f = 30. \; m = f - 4$
   c. 17   **d.** 13

 e–f. $f + m = 12. \; m = f + 2$
   e. 5   **f.** 7
   g. 12. $f = 17 - 5$ **h.** 6. $m = 13 - 7$

35. **Given:** n is a real number, $n > 0$.

  Prove: $n + \frac{1}{n} \geq 2.$

Proof: Suppose $n + \frac{1}{n} < 2$. Then $n^2 + 1 < 2n$, so $n^2 - 2n + 1 < 0$. But $n^2 - 2n + 1 = (n - 1)^2$, so $(n - 1)^2 < 0$, which is impossible, since the square of any real number is never negative. Therefore, the supposition has to be wrong, and so $n + \frac{1}{n} \geq 2$.

36. No. Lanham had them in sight for only one second, and that's a very short time to see two people for the first time and be able to identify them positively afterward. Also, their distance from Lanham was more than 77 feet at the beginning of the second and at least 40 feet at the end of the second, not to mention that he was seeing them through a windshield for part of the second. The car traveled 66 feet at 45 mph while Lanham watched.

$t = \frac{D}{r} = \frac{66 \text{ feet} \times 3{,}600 \text{ sec per hour}}{45 \text{ mph} \times 5{,}280 \text{ ft per mile}} =$

$\frac{66(3{,}600 \text{ sec})}{45(5{,}280)} = 1 \text{ sec}$

(Credit for the idea for this problem goes to a Perry Mason book, "The Case of the Waylaid Wolf," by Erle Stanley Gardner.)

37. 100; $11. $md = 1{,}100$
$(m - 12)(d + 1.50) = 1{,}100$

38. $-\frac{2}{3}$ or $\frac{3}{2}$. $\frac{n}{d} = \frac{d}{n} + \frac{5}{6}$

39. $3b + 2m + e = 5.44$
$6b + m + e = 7.12$
$2b + 2m + 3e = 6.13$
  a. 89¢   **b.** 99¢
  c. 79¢

40. $me = 14.40$
$(m + 6)(e - .12) = 14.40$
  a. 24   **b.** 60¢

41. 121 and 16. $a + b = 137$
$\sqrt{a} - \sqrt{b} = 7$

42. **a.** 1,540. $S = \frac{55(56)}{2}$

　　b. 5,050. $S = \frac{100(101)}{2}$

　　c. 125,250. $S = \frac{500(501)}{2}$

　　d. 12. $78 = \frac{n(n+1)}{2}$

　　e. 24. $300 = \frac{n(n+1)}{2}$

　　f. 49. $1,225 = \frac{n(n+1)}{2}$

　　g. 320,200. $S = \frac{1,000(1,001)}{2} - \frac{600(601)}{2}$

　　h. 8,550. $S = \frac{150(151)}{2} - \frac{74(75)}{2}$

　　i. 105,350. $S = \frac{500(501)}{2} - \frac{199(200)}{2}$

　　j. 202 through 251

　　　　$\frac{(n+50)(n+51)}{2} - \frac{n(n+1)}{2} = 11,325$

　　k. 5,005 through 5,014

　　　　$\frac{(n+10)(n+11)}{2} - \frac{n(n+1)}{2} = 50,095$

　　l. 100 through 199

　　　　$\frac{(n+100)(n+101)}{2} - \frac{n(n+1)}{2} = 14,950$

　　m. 2 through 26

　　　　$\frac{(n+25)(n+26)}{2} - \frac{n(n+1)}{2} = 350$

43. Martha is 14; Nick is 18; Perry is 17.
$M + N = 2P - 2$

$N + P = \frac{5}{2}M$

$N + 2 = 2(M - 4)$

44. $24; 30. $rh = 720$
$(r - 4)(h + 6) = 720$

45. $V = lwh$, so $V = (50 - 2h)(30 - 2h)h$.

Use synthetic division to find a rational root. Then use the quadratic formula to find the other root(s).

　　a. 2 in **or** $(19 - \sqrt{62}\,)$ in for each side. $V = 2,392$. Notice that

the other root, $19 + \sqrt{62}$, does not satisfy the conditions of the problem, since a square having a side this long would force both length and width of the box to be negative numbers.

　　b. 5 in **or** $\left(\frac{35 - 5\sqrt{17}}{2}\right)$ in for each

side. $V = 4,000$. Notice that the

other root, $\frac{35 + 5\sqrt{17}}{2}$, does not

satisfy the conditions of the problem.

46. 120 ft. The ball travels 60 feet (down) + $2(\frac{1}{3})(60)$

feet (up and down) + $2(\frac{1}{3})[(\frac{1}{3})(60)]$

feet (up and down) +...

$= 60 + 120\left(\frac{1}{3} + \frac{1}{3^2} + \frac{1}{3^3} + ...\right)$

$= 60 + 40\left(\frac{1}{3} + \frac{1}{3^2} + ...\right)$ = (using the

formula for the sum of an infinite

geometric series) $60 + 40(\frac{3}{2}) = 120$ ft.

47. **a.** $400 semiannually. The thing to realize about this problem is that the $1,000 annual raises will not amount to 5($1,000) = $5,000 total for the five years. The first raise will be $1,000, but the second raise will be an additional $1,000, or $2,000, more than the starting salary. Since the first raise will not take effect until the second year, and so on, there will be only four raises during the five-year period, and these will total $1,000(1 + 2 + 3 + 4) = $10,000. Then $20,000 salary x 5 + $10,000 raises = $110,000 total during the five-year period. Similarly, there will be nine $400 semiannual raises, and these will total $400 (1 + 2 +...+ 9) = $18,000, making a total of $118,000 in salary and raises.

b. $222.22. Since the semiannual raises, s, will total $(1 + 2 +...+ 9)s = 45s$, we need $45s = 10,000$, the total of the $1,000 raises.

48. $c + s + r = n$

$1.00c + 1.50s + 3.00r = t$

a. 100 for children, 70 for senior citizens, 50 other.
$n = 220$, $c = 2r$, $t = 355$

b. 70 for children, 140 for senior citizens, 200 other.
$n = 410$, $c = \frac{1}{2}s$, $t = 880$

c. 200 for children, 100 for senior citizens, 300 other.
$n = 600$, $r = c + s$, $t = 1,250$

d. 100 for children, 200 for senior citizens, 105 other.
$n = 405$, $r = c + 5$, $t = 715$

49. $\left(\sqrt{r^2 + 9} - r\right)$ units.

$A = \pi r^2$, so $\pi r^2 + 9\pi = \pi(r + x)^2$. (Solve for x.)

50. $C_B = 2C_A$

$P_B = S_B - C_B = \frac{3}{4}(S_A - C_A) = \frac{3}{4}P_A$

a. $1,000 for A, $2,000 for B
$C_A + C_B = 3,000$

b. $750 for A, $1,500 for B.
$1.20(C_A + C_B) = 2,700$

c. $1,480 for A, $2,360 for B.
$S_A + S_B = 3,840$

$1.28(C_A + C_B) = 3,840$

d. $5,000 for A, $5,000 for B.
$C_A + C_B = 3,000$

$.30(S_A + S_B) = 3,000$

e. $400 on A, $300 on B
$P_A + P_B = 700$

f. $800 on A, $600 on B
$S_A + S_B = 2,900$

g. $1,600 on A, $1,200 on B
$C_A + C_B = 6,000$

$S_A + S_B = 8,800$

51. Put n = no. of normal birds.

Put b = no. of birds with 2 heads and 3 legs.

Put h = no. of birds with 2 heads and (exactly) 2 legs.

Put g = no. of birds with (exactly) 1 head and 3 legs.

Then the basic system of equations is $n + b + h + g = 300$

$n + 2b + 2h + g = 315$

$2n + 3b + 2h + 3g = 690$

a. 195 normal,
0 with two heads and three legs,
15 with two heads and two legs,
90 with one head and three legs.
$b = 0$

b. 210 normal,
15 with two heads and three legs,
0 with two heads and two legs,
75 with one head and three legs.
$h = 0$

c. 200 normal,
5 with two heads and three legs,
10 with two heads and two legs,
85 with one head and three legs.
$b = 5$

d. 198 normal,
3 with two heads and three legs,

12 with two heads and two legs, 87 with one head and three legs.

$b = \frac{1}{5}(h + b)$

52. 5 in **or** $4\sqrt{5}$ in, depending on which segment is 3 in long and which one is 8 in. long. $A = ba$, so $44 = (3 + 8)a$. Then draw diagrams and use the Pythagorean Theorem.

53. $1\frac{1}{2}$ hours after the 10-inch candle was lit. The 12-inch candle had already burned $\frac{1}{2}$ of $2\frac{1}{2}$, or $1\frac{1}{4}$ inches, when the 10-inch candle was lit, so at that point the 12-inch candle was $10\frac{3}{4}$ inches long. Then $10\frac{3}{4} - (2\frac{1}{2})h$ = the 12-inch candle's length h hours after the 10-inch candle was lit, and $10 - 2h$ = the 10-inch candle's length h hours after it was lit. So the equation needed is $10\frac{3}{4} - (2\frac{1}{2})h = 10 - 2h$. An alternative equation is $12 - 2\frac{1}{2}(h + \frac{1}{2}) = 10 - 2h$.

54. **a.** 2 ft. $80(6) = 120(6 - d)$

b. Nancy, 5 ft.; Alfred, 4 ft
$80d = 100(d - 1)$

c. on Alfred's side, $1\frac{1}{2}$ ft
$120(6) = 100(6) + 80d$

d. on Homer's side, $1\frac{1}{2}f$
$100(6) = 120(4) + 80d$

e. on Homer's side, 3 feet from the fulcrum.
$80(6) = 120(\frac{3}{2}) + 100d$

f. Nancy, $2\frac{8}{9}$ ft; Alfred, $4\frac{8}{9}$ ft
$120(6) = 80d + 100(d + 2)$

g. Alfred, $3\frac{1}{9}$ ft; Nancy $5\frac{1}{9}$ ft
$120(6) = 100d + 80(d + 2)$

h. on Alfred's side, $3\frac{3}{4}$ ft from the fulcrum. $50(6) + 120(5) = 100(6) + 80d$

55. From the given information, taxes will be at these rates:

$\$0 \le$ income $\le \$2{,}000$: tax = 15% of income.

$\$2{,}000 <$ income $\le \$4{,}000$: tax = $\$300 + 18\%$ of income over $\$2{,}000$.

$\$4{,}000 <$ income $\le \$6{,}000$: tax = $\$660 + 20\%$ of income over $\$4{,}000$.

$\$6{,}000 <$ income $\le \$8{,}000$: tax = $\$1{,}060 + 25\%$ of income over $\$6{,}000$.

We use this information to simplify the problem.

Put x = income. Then

a. $\$4{,}700$
$800 = 660 + .20(x - 4{,}000)$

b. $\$7{,}100$
$1{,}335 = 1{,}060 + .25(x - 6{,}000)$

c. $\$3{,}900$
$642 = 300 + .18(x - 2{,}000)$

56. $D = rt$, $t_B = t_A - \frac{3}{4}$

a–b. $D = 200$, $r_A = 20$

a. $21\frac{23}{37}$ mph. $r = \dfrac{200}{10 - \frac{3}{4}}$

b. $66\frac{2}{3}$ miles. Put t = the no. of hours A rides before B overtakes A. Then the distance (s)he rides is $D = 20t = (\frac{800}{37})(t - \frac{1}{4})$.

c. 75 miles. $D = 20t_A = 25(t_A - \frac{3}{4})$

d. 25 miles. See b above.

$$D = 20t = 25(t - \frac{1}{4})$$

57. a. Donna is 12, Edwin is 15, Floyd is 17. $(\frac{1}{3})(D + E) = (\frac{1}{2})(F + 1)$

$$3(F - E) = \frac{1}{2}D$$

$$D + F = 2E - 1$$

b. Donna is $2\frac{2}{5}$, Edwin is 3, Floyd is $2\frac{3}{5}$. $\frac{1}{3}(D + E) = \frac{1}{2}(F + 1)$

$$3(E - F) = \frac{1}{2}D$$

$$D + F = 2E - 1$$

58. a. $D = r_A t_A = r_B(t_A - \frac{3}{4})$, so

$$r_B = \frac{r_A t_A}{t_A - \frac{3}{4}} = \frac{D}{t_A - \frac{3}{4}}$$

$D_O = r_A t = r_B(t - \frac{1}{4})$, so

$$t = \frac{1}{4}\left(\frac{r_B}{r_B - r_A}\right), \text{ and so}$$

$$D_O = \frac{1}{4}\left(\frac{r_A r_B}{r_B - r_A}\right)$$

$$= \frac{1}{4}r_A\left(\frac{\dfrac{D}{t_A - \frac{3}{4}}}{\dfrac{D}{t_A - \frac{3}{4}} - r_A}\right)$$

$$= \frac{1}{4}\left(\frac{r_A D}{D - r_A t_A + \frac{3}{4}r_A}\right)$$

$$= \frac{1}{4}\left(\frac{r_A D}{D - D + \frac{3}{4}r_A}\right) = \frac{1}{4}\left(\frac{r_A D}{\frac{3}{4}r_A}\right)$$

$$= \frac{1}{4}(\frac{4}{3})D = \frac{1}{3}D, \text{ so } D_O = \frac{1}{3}D.$$

b. See the solution for **a** above. There, B started 15 minutes, or $\frac{15}{60}$ of an hour, after A, and finished $\frac{30}{60}$ of an hour before A, giving a total of $\frac{15}{60} + \frac{30}{60} = \frac{3}{4}$ of an hour difference in time. Now we can go through the proof again, this time replacing $\frac{1}{4}$ with $\frac{a}{60}$, and replacing $\frac{3}{4}$ with $\frac{a+b}{60}$. Following all the way through to the last line, we have $D_O = \frac{a}{60}\left(\frac{a+b}{60}\right)D = \frac{a}{a+b}D$, which is the required answer.

59.

a, c. $P_q = \frac{2}{3}E_q$, $P_d = 3E_d$

$$10P_d + 25P_q - 75 = 10E_d + 25E_q$$

$$10P_d + 25P_q + 10E_d + 25E_q = 1,025$$

a. 10 dimes, 15 quarters.
b. $4.75. $10(\$.10) + 15(\$.25)$
c. 30 dimes, 10 quarters.
d. $5.50. $30(\$.10) + 10(\$.25)$

60. Given: $a + b = c + d$, $ab = cd$. Prove: Either $a = c$, $b = d$; or $a = d$, $b = c$. Proof: $a + b = c + d$, so

$$a^2 + 2ab + b^2 = c^2 + 2cd + d^2.$$

$ab = cd$, so $4ab = 4cd$. Then

$$a^2 - 2ab + b^2 = c^2 - 2cd + d^2.$$

Then $(a - b)^2 = (c - d)^2$, so $|a - b| = gh|c - d|.*$

Case I: $a > b, c > d$.
Then $a - b = c - d$ (from *)

$a + b = c + d$ (given)
So $a = c, b = d$

Case II: $a > b, c < d$.
Then $a - b = d - c$ (from *)
$a + b = c + d$ (given)
So $a = d, b = c$.

Case III: $a < b, c > d$.
Then $b - a = c - d$ (from *)
$a + b = c + d$ (given)
So $b = c, a = d$.

Case IV: $a < b, c < d$.
Then $b - a = d - c$ (from *)
$a + b = c + d$ (given)
So $b = d, a = c$.

Case V: $a = b$.
Then $c = d$ (from *)
$a + b = c + d$ (given)
So $a = c, b = d$ or $a = d, b = c$
Thus we have proved the required relationship in every case.

61. **a, c.** $5n_D + 10d_D + 25q_D = 2(5n_E + 10d_E + 25q_E)$

$n_D + d_D + q_D = (\frac{1}{2})(n_E + d_E + q_E)$

$d_D + q_D = 27$

$d_E + q_E = 6$

$n_D = \frac{1}{2} d_D$

$n_E = 10 d_E$

a. 1 nickel, 2 dimes, 25 quarters.
b. $6.50. 1($.05) + 2($.10) + 25($.25)
c. 50 nickels, 5 dimes, 1 quarter.
d. $3.25. 50($.05) + 5($.10) +

1($.25) or $(\frac{1}{2})$6.50

62. **a.** 7 units or $\sqrt{33}$ units. $s = \frac{4 + 5 + t}{2}$,
so $4\sqrt{6} =$
$$\sqrt{(\frac{9+t}{2})(\frac{9+t}{2} - 4)(\frac{9+t}{2} - 5)(\frac{9+t}{2} - t)}.$$
Inside the radical we can combine terms within each parentheses

and factor $\frac{1}{2}$ from each

parentheses and have

$(\frac{1}{16})(9 + t)(1 + t)(-1 + t)(9 - t)$ or

$(\frac{1}{16})(-t^2 + 81)(t^2 - 1)$.

Squaring both sides of the

equation, we have $96 = (\frac{1}{16})(-t^4 +$

$82t^2 - 81)$, so $t^4 - 82t^2 + 1{,}617 = 0$.
Then $(t^2 - 49)(t^2 - 33) = 0$ and,
since $t > 0$, $t = 7$ or $t = \sqrt{33}$.

b. 3, 4, and 5 units. $a + b = 7$, $b + c = 9$, $a + c = 8$. Solve the system and use Hero's formula.

c. 6 square units. $s = \frac{3 + 4 + 5}{2}$. Use Hero's formula.

d. 8, 15, and 17 units. $a + b = 23$, $b + c = 32$. Solve and get $b = 23 - a$, c

$= 9 + a$. Then $s = \frac{a + 32}{2}$, so $a = 2s -$

32. From Hero's formula, $60 =$

$\sqrt{s(s - a)[s - (23 - a)][s - (9 + a)]}$.

Substitute $2s - 32$ for a and get

$60 = \sqrt{s(-s + 32)(3s - 55)(-s + 23)}$.

Expand, square both sides, and collect terms: $3s^4 - 220s^3 + 5{,}233s^2 - 40{,}480s - 3{,}600 = 0$.

Use synthetic division to find that the only rational root is 20. (Synthetic division will also show that the other three roots lie between $-\frac{1}{3}$ and 0, 20 and 30, 30 and 36.) Since $s = \frac{a+b+c}{2} = 20$, it

is now easily found that $a = 8$, $b = 15$, $c = 17$.

63. 17. Given: $10t + u$. $10(t + 5) + (u - 2) + 10t + u = 82$, so $10(2t + 5) + 2u - 2 = 82$. Then $2u - 2 = 2$ or 12, and so $u = 2$ or 7. If $u = 2$, then $10(2t + 5) + 4 - 2 = 82$, and $20t + 50 = 80$, a contradiction. Therefore $u \neq 2$, so $u = 7$. Then $10(2t + 5) + 14 - 2 = 82$, so $20t + 50 = 70$, and so $t = 1$.

64. **a.** $1{:}05\frac{5}{11}$. $m = \frac{60(1)}{11} = 5\frac{5}{11}$

b. $2{:}10\frac{10}{11}$. $m = \frac{60(2)}{11} = 10\frac{10}{11}$

c. $6{:}32\frac{8}{11}$. $m = \frac{60(6)}{11} = 32\frac{8}{11}$

d. $9{:}49\frac{1}{11}$. $m = \frac{60(9)}{11} = 49\frac{1}{11}$

e. $m = \frac{60h}{11}$. In one hour, the minute

hand of a clock moves in a complete circle, or 360°, while the hour hand moves only from one hourly number to the next, or 30°. Two solutions to the problem are given below.

Solution 1 (using simple algebra):

This solution uses the fact that the minute hand moves 6° each minute and the hour hand moves $(\frac{1}{2})°$ each minute. Put m = the number of minutes it takes the minute hand to catch the hour hand. Then the minute hand moves $(6m)°$ in this time and the hour hand moves $(\frac{m}{2})°$ in this time. Put h = the starting hour (one, two, etc.). Then the hour hand will be $(30h)°$ ahead of the minute hand at the starting time, and the hands will coincide when they are both at the same angle—

i.e., when $30h + \frac{m}{2} = 6m$. Solving the

equation, we have $60h = 11m$ or $m = \frac{60h}{11}$.

Solution 2 (using an infinite geometric series):

This solution uses the fact that the hour hand moves at $\frac{1}{12}$th of the rate at which the minute hand moves. Put h = the starting hour (one, two, etc.). Since it takes the minute hand five minutes to reach the hour hand's starting point for one o'clock, ten minutes for two o'clock, and so on, it takes $5h$ minutes for the minute hand to reach the hour hand's starting point for any given hour h. But by the time the minute hand gets there, the hour hand has moved $\frac{1}{12}$th as far, or $\frac{5h}{12}$. And by the time the minute hand reaches this new point, the hour hand has moved $\frac{1}{12}$th of $\frac{5h}{12}$, or $\frac{5h}{12^2}$. And so on. So we have the infinite geometric series $5h + \frac{5h}{12} + \frac{5h}{12^2} + \dots$. Applying the formula for the sum of such a series, we have a sum of $\frac{5h}{1 - \frac{1}{12}}$, or $\frac{5h}{\frac{11}{12}}$, or $\frac{60h}{11}$. Since this sum is the number of minutes needed for the minute hand to catch the hour hand, we have $m = \frac{60h}{11}$. Notice that the time for eleven o'clock works out to 60 minutes, or one full hour, thus showing that the clock's hands never coincide between eleven and twelve o'clock.

(It is, of course, comforting to know that the result of our mathematical expertise agrees with what we already knew.)

65. Given: $a + b = c + d$, $ac = bd \neq 0$.
Prove: $a = d$, $b = c$.
Proof: $ac = bd$ (given), so $\frac{ac}{dc} = \frac{bd}{dc}$,

and so $\frac{a}{d} = \frac{b}{c}$, so $\frac{a+b}{d+c} = \frac{b}{c}$.

(Proof below, in case the students are unfamiliar with the theorem that allows that last step.) But $a + b$

$= c + d$ (given), so $1 = \frac{b}{c}$, and so $b = c$,

and so (from the first item given) $a = d$. Proof of the theorem, "If two ratios are equal, then the sum of their numerators is to the sum of their denominators as either numerator is to its denominator":

Given: $\frac{a}{d} = \frac{b}{c}$. Prove: $\frac{a+b}{d+c} = \frac{a}{d} = \frac{b}{c}$.

Proof: Put $r = \frac{b}{c}$. Then $r = \frac{a}{d}$, so

$a = dr$ and $b = cr$. Then $a + b = dr +$

$cr = r(c + d)$, so $\frac{a+b}{c+d} = r = \frac{a}{d} = \frac{b}{c}$.

DIOPHANTINE PROBLEMS (pp. 67-97)

A Diophantine problem is usually defined as a system of indeterminate equations having integral coefficients and integral (some definitions specify rational) solutions. Although not all equations given for solutions of the problems in this book have integral coefficients, the coefficients can be made integral by multiplying through by a common denominator. Stress to the students that answers are always whole numbers, even though fractions may appear in the problem. Zero may or may not be permissible as an answer. (If we are told there are some of each thing, then

zero cannot be an answer for one of the things.)

Along that same line, the students will probably need to be reminded that when they are told to "find all possible solutions" and they correctly find only nonnegative integral solutions (because other solutions are not acceptable for these problems), the same equation or system of equations would ordinarily produce an infinite number of solutions.

In most cases there are several of a given kind of problem, thus allowing you to do one as an example for the class if you should wish to do so.

In order to anticipate possible trouble spots and help judge how much time will be needed to find a full solution, do solve each problem yourself (looking in this section only as a last resort) before assigning it to the class.

Insist that your students check every solution (and show their work for the checks). The checks were not shown in the book along with the explanations, but this was simply because of space limitations.

A knowledge of linear congruences eliminates a good deal of the work in solving the kinds of problems given here, and you might like to encourage advanced students to acquire a working knowledge of linear congruences and apply it to the solution of Diophantine problems. In effect, the discussion on page 90 applies such knowledge, but not in as neat a way as working directly with $8t = 65 \pmod{81}$.

1. No. The definition says a prime number has to be > 1.

2. yes, yes, yes, no, no, yes, yes

3. yes, yes, yes, no, no, yes, yes

4. yes, yes, yes, no, no, yes, yes

5. yes, no; 1, 2, 3, 6;
no: 1, 3, 5, 15; yes; yes;
no: 1, 5, 13, 65

6. 2, 5; 2, 2, 3; 2, 2, 2, 2; 2, 3, 3; 2, 5, 5; 2, 3, 5

7. no, 2; yes; no, 4; no, 2; no, 3; no, 3; no, 2

8. $a = 2b$; $2c = 3d$; $11e = 2f$; $g = 2(h + j)$; $2k = 5m - 4n$; $2p + 5 = 3q - 1$

9. **a.** $a = 1, b = 1.$ $a = \frac{9 - 7b}{2}$

   b. $(a, b) = (3, 4), (0, 9).$ $a = \frac{3(9 - b)}{2}$

   c. $(a, b) = (1, 15), (3, 10), (5, 5),$

   $(7, 0).$ $b = \frac{5(7 - a)}{2}$

10. **a.** $(c, d) = (1, 1).$ $c = \frac{11 - 6d}{5}$

   b. $(c, d) = (1, 2), (6, 0).$ $d = \frac{2(6 - c)}{5}$

   c. $(c, d) = (6, 1), (3, 3), (0, 5).$

   $c = \frac{3(5 - d)}{2}$

   d. $(c, d) = (3, 4).$ $d = \frac{2(19 - 3c)}{5}$

11. **a.** $(f, g) = (3, 10), (9, 5), (15, 0).$

   $g = \frac{5(15 - f)}{6}$

   b. $(f, g) = (0, 12), (5, 8), (10, 4),$

   $(15, 0).$ $f = \frac{5(12 - g)}{4}$ or $g = \frac{4(15 - f)}{5}$

   c. $(f, g) = (1, 5), (3, 0).$ $g = \frac{5(3 - f)}{2}$

12. **a.** $(a, b, c) = (96, 3, 1), (97, 1, 2)$
   $b + 2c = 5$

   b. $(c, d, e) = (0, 10, 40), (1, 8, 41),$
   $(2, 6, 42), (3, 4, 43), (4, 2, 44),$
   $(5, 0, 45).$ $d = 2(5 - c)$

   c. $(f, g, h) = (0, 3, 91), (1, 2, 92),$
   $(2, 1, 93), (3, 0, 94).$ $g = 3 - f$

   d. $(j, k, m) = (92, 0, 2), (94, 1, 1),$
   $(96, 2, 0).$ $k = 2 - m$

e. $(m, p, q) = (85, 15, 0), (89, 10, 1),$
   $(93, 5, 2), (97, 0, 3).$ $p = 5(3 - q)$

f. $(a, b, c) = (0, 20, 8), (1, 25, 4),$
   $(2, 30, 0).$ $c = 4(2 - a)$

13.

	plane	car	
a.	1	8	
	2	6	
	3	4	
	4	2	$10p + 5c = 50$
b.	2	10	
	6	5	$5p + 4c = 50$
c.	2	15	
	8	10	
	14	5	$2.50p + 3c = 50$
d.	4	8	$4.50p + 4c = 50$
e.	2	12	
	5	5	$7p + 3c = 50$
f.	15	2	
	10	4	
	5	6	$2.50p + 6.25c = 50$

14. 14 toasters and 30 broilers; **or** 31 toasters and 20 broilers; **or** 48 toasters and 10 broilers.
$17b + 10t = 650$

15. $A + B + C = 100$

	A	B	C	
a.	90	10	0	
	91	8	1	
	92	6	2	
	93	4	3	
	94	2	4	
	95	0	5	$2A + 3B + 4C = 210$
b.	96	2	2	
	95	5	0	$2A + 4B + 5C = 210$

	A	B	C
c.	90	10	0
	92	7	1
	94	4	2
	96	1	3

$2A + 3B + 5C = 210$

	A	B	C
d.	90	10	0
	93	6	1
	96	2	2

$2A + 3B + 6C = 210$

	A	B	C
e.	95	5	0
	96	3	1
	97	1	2

$2A + 4B + 6C = 210$

	A	B	C
f.	82	2	16
	79	9	12
	76	16	8
	73	23	4
	70	30	0

$1.50A + 3.50B + 5C = 210$

	A	B	C
g.	84	2	14
	82	11	7
	80	20	0

$1.75A + 3.50B + 4C = 210$

	A	B	C
h.	75	22	3
	80	8	12

$1.50A + 3.75B + 5C = 210$

16.

	n	d	h
	80	20	0
	88	11	1
	96	2	2

$n + d + h = 100$
$5n + 10d + 50h = 600$

17. $p + s + c = 100$

	p	s	c
a.	9	1	90

$5p + 10s + \frac{1}{2}c = 100$

	p	s	c
b.	10	2	88

$4p + 8s + \frac{1}{2}c = 100$

	p	s	c
c.	7	1	92

$7p + 5s + \frac{1}{2}c = 100$

	p	s	c
d.	5	3	92

$6p + 8s + \frac{1}{2}c = 100$

	p	s	c
e.	0	4	96

$5p + 13s + \frac{1}{2}c = 100$

	p	s	c
f.	30	2	68
	25	5	70
	20	8	72
	15	11	74
	10	14	76
	5	17	78
	0	20	80

$2p + 3s + \frac{1}{2}c = 100$

18.

p	n	d
85	7	8
80	16	4
75	25	0

$p + n + d = 100$
$1p + 5n + 10d = 200$

19.

r	s	c
0	50	50
2	45	53
4	40	56
6	35	59
8	30	62
10	25	65
12	20	68
14	15	71
16	10	74
18	5	77
20	0	80

$r + s + c = 100$
$3r + 1.50s + .50c = 100$

20. $a + p + g = 70$

	a	p	g
a.	2	2	66

$10a + 14p + \frac{1}{3}g = 70$

	a	p	g
b.	2	4	64

$7a + 10p + \frac{1}{4}g = 70$

	a	p	g
c.	6	1	63

$\frac{20}{3}a + 9p + \frac{1}{3}g = 70$

d. 8 2 60

$$5a + p + \frac{1}{4}g = 70$$

e. 8 7 55
20 0 50

$$3a + 5p + \frac{1}{5}g = 70$$

f. 4 15 51
12 10 48
20 5 45
28 0 42

$$2a + 3p + \frac{1}{3}g = 70$$

g. 1 12 57
12 4 54

$$3a + 4p + \frac{1}{3}g = 70$$

21. 20 sold, regular price $10 **or** 40 sold, regular price $5.
$.25t(.80p) + .75tp = 190$

22. $x^2 - y^2 = D$, so $(x - y)(x + y) = D$. The problem then becomes very simple to solve, for we merely have to try all possible pairs of factors of D, using the smaller factor for $x - y$, and the larger factor for $x + y$. Then $2x =$ the sum of the factors. For example, if $D = 15$, then the factors are 1 and 15, or 3 and 5. Then $x - y = 1$, $x + y = 15$, $2x = 16$, $x = 8$, and $y = 7$. Or $x - y = 3$, $x + y = 5$, $2x = 8$, $x = 4$, and $y = 1$.

a. 11 and 9; 7 and 3. $D = 40 = 1(40) = 2(20) = 4(10) = 5(8)$

b. 11 and 10; 5 and 2.
$D = 21 = 1(21) = 3(7)$

c. 13 and 11; 8 and 4; 7 and 1.
$D = 48 = 1(48) = 2(24) = 3(16) = 4(12) = 6(8)$

d. 28 and 26; 12 and 6. $D = 108 = 1(108) = 2(54) = 3(36) = 4(27) = 6(18) = 9(12)$

e. 19 and 17; 11 and 7; 9 and 3. $D = 72 = 1(72) = 2(36) = 3(24) = 4(18) = 6(12) = 8(9)$

f. 29 and 27; 16 and 12; 11 and 3. $D = 112 = 1(112) = 2(56) = 4(28) = 7(16) = 8(14)$

23. 8 (5 in the first batch, 3 in the second) **or** 16 (10 in the first batch, 6 in the second).
$82f + 90s = 85(f + s)$

24.

n	d	q	
80	20	0	
83	16	1	
86	12	2	
89	8	3	
92	4	4	
95	0	5	$n + d + q = 100$

$5n + 10d + 25q = 600$

25. $A = \frac{ab}{2}$, $a^2 + b^2 = c^2$

A is given, and $ab = 2A$, so all possibilities for a and b can be discovered by factoring $2A$. It then becomes a matter of using these factors in the Pythagorean Theorem and determining whether or not c^2 is prime.

a. 3 and 4. $A = 6 = 1(6) = 2(3)$

b. 1 and 24 **or** 3 and 8
$A = 12 = 1(12) = 2(6) = 3(4)$

c. 2 and 35 **or** 7 and 10
$A = 35 = 1(35) = 5(7)$

d. No solution. (No c^2 is prime.)
$A = 100 = 1(100) = 2(50) = 4(25) = 5(20) = 10(10)$

e. 1 and 40 **or** 5 and 8
$A = 20 = 1(20) = 2(10) = 4(5)$

f. 1 and 420 **or** 3 and 140 **or** 15 and 28. $A = 210 = 1(210) = 2(105) = 3(70) = 5(42) = 6(35) = 7(30) = 10(21) = 14(15)$

26. There are seven ways.

a	b	c
40	20	40
42	21	37
44	22	34
46	23	31
48	24	28
50	25	25
52	26	22

$a + b + c = 100$
$a = 2b$
$a, b, c \geq 20$

27. $10h + .15e = T$

a. 1 lot, 100 individual. $T = 25$

b. 0 lots, 210 individual **or** 3 lots, 10 individual. $T = 31.50$

c. 0 lots, 400 individual **or** 3 lots, 200 individual **or** 6 lots, 0 individual. $T = 60$

d. 0 lots, 500 individual **or** 3 lots, 300 individual **or** 6 lots, 100 individual. $T = 75$

28. We have to remember to count everything that applies. For example, birds have a total of five wings, legs, and heads.

a. 14 birds, 2 cows, 6 men. (**Not** 15 birds, 5 cows, 0 men, since we're given that there were some men there.).
$3b + m + c = 50$
$3b + 3m + 5c = 70$

b. 6 men and any combination of birds and cows totaling 25, except that zero is not allowed.
$5b + 3m + 5c = 134$
$4b + 2m + 4c = 106$

c. 18 birds, 3 cows, 3 men **or** 17 birds, 2 cows, 7 men **or** 16 birds, 1 cow, 11 men. $3b + m + c = 60$
$4b + 2m + 4c = 90$

d. 8 birds, 7 men, 1 cow **or** 9 birds, 1 man, 4 cows. $3b + 3m + 5c = 50$
$3b + m + c = 32$

e. 4 birds, 1 cow, 5 men.
$5b + 3m + 5c = 40$
$3b + 3m + 5c = 32$

29. This one is worked in exactly the same way as problem **22.** $c^2 - b^2 = a^2$, so $(c - b)(c + b) = a^2$.

a.

hyp	leg
17	15
10	6

$a = 8$.
$64 = 1(64) = 2(32) = 4(16) = 8(8)$

b.

hyp	leg
145	143
74	70
51	45
40	32
30	18
26	10
25	7

$a = 24$. $576 = 1(576) = 2(288) = 3(192) = 4(144) = 6(96) = 8(72) = 9(64) = 12(48) = 16(36) = 18(32) = 24(24)$

c.

61	60

$a = 11$. $121 = 1(121) = 11(11)$

d.

1013	1012
339	336
205	200
117	108
75	60
53	28
51	24

$a = 45$. $2025 = 1(2025) = 3(675) = 5(405) = 9(225) = 15(135) = 25(81) = 27(75) = 45(45)$

e. 82   80
    30   24
$a = 18$. $324 = 1(324) = 2(162) =$
$3(108) = 4(81) = 6(54) = 9(36) =$
$12(27) = 18(18)$

30. All fractions having all four digits
the same, as well as the fractions

$\frac{16}{64}, \frac{19}{95}, \frac{26}{65}$, and $\frac{49}{98}$. (There is probably
a nontedious way to do this problem,
but I didn't find it. I set the
product of the means equal to the
product of the extremes, combined
the two *hy* terms, and then selected
one variable to be held constant in
order to have an equation in only two
variables—e.g., set $h = 1$, solve
the resulting equation for either u
or y, find all solutions, then set $h = 2$
and go through it all again, and so on
through $h = 9$.)

31. All fractions having all four digits
the same, as well as the fractions

$\frac{64}{16}, \frac{65}{26}, \frac{95}{19}$, and $\frac{98}{49}$. Inverting the
fractions found for problem **30** will
work, but if the students insist on

having an equation, $\frac{10h + u}{10y + h} = \frac{u}{y}$.

32. (Draw a diagram.) Let $2a$ and $2b$
be the diagonals, s be the side of
the rhombus. Then the rhombus is
divided into four congruent right
triangles having legs a and b and
hypotenuse s, so $a^2 + b^2 = s^2$. Also,
given in the problem that $A =$

$(2a)(2b) = 2ab$. Then $(a + b)2 = s^2 +$

$\frac{1}{2} A$, and $(a - b)2 = s^2 - A$, so $A = (a + b)^2 - s^2 = s^2 - (a - b)^2$, so $A = (a + b - s)(a + b + s) = (s + b - a)(s + a - b)$.
Then the object is to factor A into
two pairs of factors satisfying the
equation. (Notice that the highest
factor used must be for $a + b + s$,

thus cutting down on guesswork.)
It will be convenient in each part
of the problem to ignore pairs of
factors that have different parity.

(1) If such a pair is used for
$(s + b - a)(s + a - b)$, then we would
have $2s =$ an odd number and so s
would not be integral.

(2) If such a pair is used for
$(a + b - s)(a + b + s)$, then we would
have $2(a + b) =$ an odd number, and
so $a + b$ would not be integral. Then
$(a + b)^2 = a^2 + 2ab + b^2 = a^2 + b^2 +$
A would not be integral. But A is
given as integral in each part of the
problem, so it follows that $a^2 + b^2$
would not be integral. But, $a^2 + b^2 = s^2$,
and if s^2 is not an integer, then s is
not an integer. Consequently, we can
ignore all pairs of factors that have
different parity.*

a. side   diagonal
   5   6 and 8.
   $24 = 1(24) = 2(12) = 3(8) = 4(6)$.
   From *, we can ignore the first
   and third pairs of factors. Then
   we must have $a + b - s = 2$, $a + b + s = 12$, $s + b - a = 4$ (or 6), and $s + a - b = 6$ (or 4). Solving, we get $s = 5$, $a = 4$ (or 3), $b = 3$ (or 4). So
   the side of the rhombus is 5, and
   its diagonals are 2(3) and 2(4), or
   6 and 8. We have now eliminated
   all possible pairs of factors of
   24, so this is the only solution.

b. side   diagonal
   26   20 and 48.
   $480 = 1(480) = 2(240) = 3(160) = 4(120) = 5(96) = 6(80) = 8(60) = 10(48) = 12(40) = 15(32) = 16(30) = 20(24)$. From *, we ignore all
   pairs of factors of different
   parity. Proceeding as in part a, we
   find initially that $a + b$ can be any
   of 161, 62, 43, 34, 29, 26, and

23, while s can be any of 62, 43, 34, 29, 26, 23, and 22. But the only combination giving $(a + b)^2 - s^2 = A$ is $a + b = 34$, $s = 26$. Solving, we get $a = 10$ (or 24), $b = 24$ (or 10).

c–e. The problems are solved in the same way as outlined above. Pairs of factors containing only one odd number have been eliminated. Pairs of factors are:

c.
side	diagonal
122	44 and 240
73	96 and 110

(for 5280): 2, 2640; 4, 1320; 6, 880; 8, 660; 10, 528; 12, 440; 16, 330; 20, 264; 22, 240; 24, 220; 30, 176; 40, 132; 44, 120; 48, 110; 60, 88; 66, 80.

d.
side	diagonal
74	48 and 140
113	30 and 224
58	80 and 84

(for 3360): 2, 1680; 4, 840; 6, 560; 8, 420; 10, 336; 12, 280; 14, 240; 16, 210; 20, 168; 24, 140; 28, 120; 30, 112; 40, 84; 42, 80; 48, 70; 56, 60.

e.
side	diagonal
365	54 and 728
255	78 and 504

(for 19,656): 2, 9828; 4, 4914; 6, 3276; 12, 1638; 14, 1404; 18, 1092; 26, 756; 28, 702; 36, 546; 42, 468; 52, 378; 54, 364; 78, 252; 84, 234; 108, 182; 126, 156.

33.
regular	discount

$25r + 30(.90d) = t$

a. $7 $8 $t = 391$

b. $6 $12 $t = 474$

c. $35 $5
   $8 $30 $t = 1010$

34.
A	B	C
16	21	63
12	22	66
8	23	69
4	24	72
0	25	75

$A + B + C = 100$

$A + 2B + \frac{2}{3}C = 100$

$A < 20$

35. $t + c + s = 100$

a. $\frac{1}{3}t + 4c + 5s = 100$

b. $\frac{1}{4}t + 3c + 5s = 100$

36. $A + B + C + D = 100$
$D < 10$

A	B	C	D
a. 13	26	52	9
14	28	56	2

$A = \frac{1}{2}B$, $C = 4A$

| b. 16 | 32 | 48 | 4 |

$A = \frac{1}{2}B$, $C = 3A$

| c. 21 | 28 | 42 | 9 |

$A = \frac{1}{2}C$, $B = \frac{2}{3}C$

| d. 22 | 11 | 66 | 1 |

$A = 2B$, $A = \frac{1}{3}C$

| e. 24 | 32 | 36 | 8 |

$A = \frac{3}{4}B$, $A = \frac{2}{3}C$

| f. 36 | 36 | 27 | 1 |

$A = B = \frac{4}{3}C$

37. $t + c + s = 100$

t	c	s
a. 64	32	4

$$\frac{76 \quad 13 \quad 11}{t + 2c + 5s = 100}$$

b. $86 \quad 9 \quad 5$
$80 \quad 20 \quad 0$
$t + 3c + 6s = 100$

38. Following is a general proof for the case of s survivors, which takes care of part **e** of the problem. Computations for parts **a–d** use the formula developed here and appear after this proof. The general formula given as a hint in the problem is used below in order to simplify unwieldy expressions.

Put S_k = the kth survivor, t = the total number of coconuts gathered.

S_1 discarded 1, leaving $t - 1$. He took $\frac{t-1}{s}$, leaving $\frac{(s-1)(t-1)}{s}$.

S_2 discarded 1, leaving $\frac{(s-1)(t-1)-s}{s}$.

He took $\frac{(s-1)(t-1)-s}{s^2}$, leaving

$\frac{(s-1)^2(t-1)-s(s-1)}{s^2}$.

S_3 discarded 1, leaving

$\frac{(s-1)^2(t-1)-s(s-1)-s^2}{s^2}$. He took

$\frac{(s-1)^2(t-1)-s(s-1)-s^2}{s^3}$, leaving

$\frac{(s-1)^3(t-1)-s(s-1)^2-s^2(s-1)}{s^3}$. We see now

a general pattern showing that for all k, S_k discarded 1, leaving

$$\frac{(s-1)^{k-1}(t-1)-s(s-1)^{k-2}-s^2(s-1)^{k-3}-\ldots s^{k-2}(s-1)-s^{k-1}}{s^{k-1}}$$

$$= \frac{(s-1)^{k-1}(t-1)+(s-1)^{k-1}-\left[s(s-1)^{k-2}+s^2(s-1)^{k-3}+\cdots s^{k-2}(s-1)+s^{k-1}\right]}{s^{k-1}}$$

= (from the formula given as a hint)

$$\frac{(s-1)^{k-1}(t-1)-(s-1)^{k-1}-\frac{(s-1)^k-s^k}{(s-1)-s}}{s^{k-1}} =$$

$$\frac{(s-1)^{k-1}(t-1)+(s-1)^{k-1}+(s-1)^k-s^k}{s^{k-1}} =$$

$$\frac{(s-1)^{k-1}(t-1)-s^k+(s-1)^{k-1}(1+s-1)}{s^{k-1}} =$$

$$\frac{(s-1)^{k-1}(t-1)-s^k+s(s-1)^{k-1}}{s^{k-1}} =$$

$$\frac{(s-1)^{k-1}(t-1+s)-s^k}{s^{k-1}}. \ \#$$

Proof (by mathematical induction) that expression # holds for all k:

S_1 discarded 1, leaving $t - 1 =$

$\frac{1(t-1+s)-s}{1} = \frac{(s-1)^{1-1}(t-1+s)-s^1}{s^{1-1}}$, which is

expression # for $k = 1$. Therefore there is an n such that # holds for

n. Then S_n took $\frac{1}{s}$ of #, or

$\frac{(s-1)^{n-1}(t-1+s)-s^n}{s^{(n-1)+1}}$, leaving

$\frac{(s-1)\left[(s-1)^{n-1}(t-1+s)-s^n\right]}{s^n} =$

$\frac{(s-1)^n(t-1+s)-s^n(s-1)}{s^n}$.

Then S_{n+1} discarded 1, leaving

$\frac{(s-1)^n(t-1+s)-s^n(s-1)-s^n}{s^n} =$

$\frac{(s-1)^n(t-1+s)-s^n(s-1+1)}{s^n} =$

$\frac{(s-1)^{(n+1)-1}(t-1+s)-s^{n+1}}{s^{(n+1)-1}}$, thus showing that if # holds for n, then # holds for $(n + 1)$. Therefore, for all k, # is the amount discarded by S_k.

The work in the proof above also shows that S_k took $\frac{(s-1)^{(k-1)}(t-1+s)-s^k}{s^k}$ and left $\frac{(s-1)^k(t-1+s)-s^k(s-1)}{s^k}$. *

38. In particular, S_s left

$\frac{(s-1)^s(t-1+s)-s^s(s-1)}{s^s}$ to be equally

distributed the next day. One coconut was discarded, and everyone got $\frac{1}{s}$ of the remainder, thus giving everyone an additional

$$\frac{(s-1)^s(t-1+s)-s^s(s+1)}{s^{s+1}}. \quad **$$

So for all k, S_k got a total of

$$\frac{(s-1)^{k-1}(t-1+s)-s^k}{s^k} + \frac{(s-1)^s(t-1+s)-s^{s+1}}{s^{s+1}} =$$

$$\frac{s^{s+1-k}(s-1)^{k-1}(t-1+s)-s^{s+1}+(s-1)^s(t-1+s)-s^{s-1}}{s^{s+1}}$$

$$= \frac{(t-1+s)(s-1)^{k-1}[s^{s+1-k}+(s-1)^{s+1-k}]-2s^{s+1}}{s^{s+1}}. \quad ***$$

An examination of the various expressions will show that if * and ** are both whole numbers, then all other expressions are also whole numbers, so the problem is reduced to finding the least t such that * and ** are both whole numbers and such that ** is not zero (imposed as a condition of the problem).

For **, put $(s-1)^s(t-1+s)-s^{s+1} = m_0 s^s + 1$. Then $(s-1)^s(t-1+s) = (m_0+1)s^s+1 = $ (put $m_0+1=m_1$)$m_1 s^{s+1}$.

Since $(s-1)$ and s are mutually prime, it has to be true that $(s-1)^s$ is a factor of m_1. So put $m_1 = m(s-1)^s$. Then $t-1+s = ms^{s+1}$, and $t = (1-s) + ms^{s+1}$.

We want a minimum value for t, so we put $m = 1$, thus having $t = 1 - s + s^{s+1}$.

Substituting this value of t in * and in ** will show that both * and ** are forced to be whole numbers, and thus the problem is solved. (Using this value of t when $s = 2$, however, makes ** $= 0$, which is not allowed, so for this one case, put $m = 2$, and have $t = 1 - s + 2s^{s+1}$.)

Since we have now determined the value for t, we can substitute this value in ***, simplifying the work of computing each survivor's total.

Then the total for $S_k = (s-1)^{k-1}[s^{s+1-k}+(s-1)^{s+1-k}]-2$, except that

if $s = 2$, then $S_k = 2(s-1)^k[s^{s+1-k}+(s-1)^{s+1-k}]-2$. And of course the number of coconuts discarded is always $s+1$.

a. 15 total; 8 for #1; 4 for #2; 3 discarded. $s = 2$, so $t = 1 - 2 + 2(2^3) = 15$.
Discarded $= 2 + 1 = 3$.
S_1 got $2(1)(2^2+1)-2 = 8$.
S_2 got $2(1)(2^1+1)-2 = 4$.

b. 79 total; 33 for #1; 24 for #2; 18 for #3; 4 discarded. $S = 3$, So $t = 1 - 3 + 3^4 = 79$.
Discarded $= 3 + 1 = 4$.
S_1 got $2^0(3^3+2^3)-2 = 79$.
S_2 got $2^1(3^2+2^2)-2 = 24$.
S_3 got $2^2(3^1+2^1)-2 = 18$.

c. 1,021 total; 335 for #1; 271 for #2; 223 for #3; 187 for #4; 5 discarded. $S = 4$, So $t = 1 - 4 + 4^5 = 1,021$.
Discarded $= 4 + 1 = 5$.
S_1 got $3^0(4^4+3^4)-2 = 335$.
S_2 got $3^1(4^3+3^3)-2 = 271$.
S_3 got $3^2(4^2+3^2)-2 = 223$.
S_4 got $3^3(4^1+3^1)-2 = 187$.

d. 15,621 total; 4,147 for #1; 3,522 for #2; 3,022 for #3; 2,522 for #4; 2,302 for #5; 6 discarded. $S = 5$, So $t = 1 - 5 + 5^6 = 15,621$.
Discarded $= 5 + 1 = 6$.
S_1 got $4^0(5^5+4^5)-2 = 4,147$.
S_2 got $4^1(5^4+4^4)-2 = 3,522$.
S_3 got $4^2(5^3+4^3)-2 = 3,022$.
S_4 got $4^3(5^2+4^2)-2 = 2,622$.
S_5 got $4^4(5^1+4^1)-2 = 2,302$.

39. a. 2,520. This is a simple version of a type of problem that has been around at least since the time of Diophantus. Here, we merely have to find the smallest number that has 5, 6, 7, 8, 9, and 10 as factors. To do this, we list the

prime factors of each number, and we strike any factor already listed.
Example: 6 = 2(3), and 8 = 2(2)(2).

One factor of 2 was already listed for 6, so for 8 we list only the additional two factors of 2. Altogether, then, we have 5[2(3)](7)[2(2)](3) = 2,520 as the least number that is divisible by 5, 6, 7, 8, 9, and 10.

b. 2,520. As a general solution, put p = the number of people who are to share their dates on any given day—i.e., 5 the second day, 6 the third day, and so on, in this problem. Then on that day the total, t, of dates has already been divided among p people,

giving each one $\frac{t}{p}$ dates. On that day, each of the p people must share with the newcomer by

dividing his $\frac{t}{p}$ dates by $p + 1$. So

the newcomer gets $p \cdot \frac{t}{p(p+1)} = \frac{t}{p+1}$

dates, and each of the other p

survivors is left with $\frac{t}{p} - \frac{t}{p(p+1)} =$

$\frac{t}{p+1}$ dates, the same number as in part **a**.

c. 2,515. We have the following information for each of the six days, where ni = the number of dates in each pile on day (i + 1):

$n_0 = \frac{t}{5}$, $n_1 = \frac{t-1}{6}$, $n_2 = \frac{t-2}{7}$,..., $n_5 = \frac{t-5}{10}$.

Solving for t, we have $t = 5n_0 = 6n_1 + 1 = 7n_2 + 2 = 8n_3 + 3 = 9n_4 + 4 = 10n_5 + 5$.

The manipulations needed are more obvious if linear congruences are used, but since the students are probably not familiar with these, the solution below does not use them. The variables a, b, c, and d are used below only as arbitrary variables to simplify the expressions.

$t = 5n_0 = 6n_1 + 1$, so $25n_0 = 30n_1 + 5$, and $n_0 = 30n_1 - 24n_0 + 5 = 6(5n_1 - 4n_0) + 5$, so $n_0 = 6a + 5$.

Then $t = 5(6a + 5) = 30a + 25 = 7n_2 + 2$. Then $120a = 28n_2 - 92$, and $a = 28n_2 - 119a - 92 = 7(4n_2 - 17a - 13) - 1 = 7b - 1 = a$.

Then $t = 30(7b - 1) + 25 = 210b - 5 = 8n_3 + 3$. Then $105b = 4n_3 + 4$, and $b = 4n_3 + 4 - 104b = 4n_3 + 1 - 26b) = 4c$.

Then $t = 210(4c) - 5 = 840c - 5 = 9n_4 + 4$.

Then $280c = 3n_4 + 3$, and $c = 3(n_4 + 1 - 93c) = 3d$.

Then $t = 840(3d) - 5 = 2,520d - 5 = 10n_5 + 5$. So $252d = n_5 + 1$. Since the coefficient of n_5 is 1, this equation does not affect the solution.

So $t = 2,520d - 5$. Since $d = 1$ will give the least value of t, we have $t = 2,515$. We can see that 2,515

is a solution by verifying that $\frac{2,515}{5}$, $\frac{2,514}{6}$, $\frac{2,513}{7}$, $\frac{2,512}{8}$, $\frac{2,511}{9}$ and $\frac{2,510}{10}$ are all whole numbers. When solving a problem of this type, it is important to manipulate the substituted variables (a, b, etc.) so that their coefficients will agree with the coefficient of the given variable.

For example, the coefficient of n_1 was 6, so the coefficient of a needed to be 6. Similarly, both b and n_2 had coefficients of 7. For c and n_3, the coefficient needed was reduced from 8 to 4 by dividing both sides of the equation by 2 before starting to manipulate any variable.

d. 2,516. This one is so easy that it is almost confusing. Everything is the same as for **c**, except they started out with one extra date, so 2,515 + 1 = 2,516.

e. 27,715. This solution uses the solution for **c**, starting after $t = 2{,}520d - 5$. $t = 5n_0 = 6n_1 + 1 = \ldots = 10n_5 + 5 = 11n_6 + 6$, so $t = 2{,}520d - 5 = 11n_6 + 6$, so $2{,}520d = 11n_6 + 11$, and $d = 11(n_6 + 1 - 229d) = 11e$.

Then $t = 2{,}520(11e) - 5 = 27{,}720e - 5$. The smallest solution is for $e = 1$, so $t = 27{,}715$. We see that 27,715 is a solution by observing

that $\frac{27{,}715}{5}$, $\frac{27{,}714}{6}$, $\frac{27{,}713}{7}$, $\frac{27{,}712}{8}$, $\frac{27{,}711}{9}$, $\frac{27{,}710}{10}$, and $\frac{27{,}709}{11}$ are all

whole numbers.

f. 2,520. The prime factors appear the same number of times in the numbers 1 through 10 as they do in the numbers 5 through 10, so the answer here is the same as the answer for **a**: 2,520.

40. $t + c + s = 100$

	t	c	s
a.	90	6	4

$\frac{1}{3}t + 5c + 10s = 100$

b.	60	39	1

$\frac{1}{4}t + 2c + 7s = 100$

c.	80	12	8

41. e. (Answers for **a–d** use the formula developed here.)

The first day, each woman had $\frac{t}{s}$, ate $\frac{1}{s}$ of $\frac{t}{s}$, and left $\frac{s-1}{s} \cdot \frac{t}{s}$.

The first night, the $(s + 1)$st survivor took $\frac{1}{s+1}$ of $\frac{s-1}{s} \cdot \frac{t}{s}$ from each pile, leaving $\frac{s}{s+1} \cdot \frac{s-1}{s} \cdot \frac{t}{s} = \frac{s-1}{s+1} \cdot \frac{t}{s}$ in each pile, and having $s(\frac{1}{s+1})(\frac{s-1}{s})\frac{t}{s} = \frac{s-1}{s+1} \cdot \frac{t}{s}$ for herself.

The second day, the $(s + 1)$ survivors gathered and divided t bananas, so each woman's total was $\frac{s-1}{s+1} \cdot \frac{t}{s} + \frac{t}{s+1} = \frac{2s-1}{s+1} \cdot \frac{t}{s}$.

Each woman ate $\frac{1}{2s}$ of $\frac{2s-1}{s+1} \cdot \frac{t}{s}$, leaving her with $\frac{2s-1}{2s} \cdot \frac{2s-1}{s+1} \cdot \frac{t}{s}$.

The second night, the $(s + 2)$nd survivor took $\frac{1}{s+2}$ of $\frac{2s-1}{2s} \cdot \frac{2s-1}{s+1} \cdot \frac{t}{s}$ bananas from each pile, leaving $\frac{s+1}{s+2} \cdot \frac{2s-1}{2s} \cdot \frac{2s-1}{s+1} \cdot \frac{t}{s} = \frac{(2s-1)^2 t}{2s^2(s+2)}$ bananas in each pile, and having the same number for herself.

The third day, the $(s + 2)$ survivors gathered t bananas, each taking $\frac{t}{s+2}$, making a total for each of $\frac{(2s-1)^2t}{2s^2(s+2)} + \frac{t}{s+2} =$

$\frac{t}{s+2}\left(\frac{6s^2-4s+1}{2s^2}\right)$ bananas. They

then ate $\frac{1}{3s}$ of these from each

pile, leaving $\frac{3s-1}{3s} \cdot \frac{t}{s+2} \cdot \frac{6s^2-4s+1}{2s^2}$

bananas in each of $(s+2)$ piles.

According to the conditions stated, we must be able to have integral answers for all of the following:

First day: $\frac{t}{s^2}$

First night: $\frac{s-1t}{s^2(s+1)}$

Second day: $\frac{t}{s+1}$ and $\frac{(2s-1)t}{2s^2(s+1)}$

Second night: $\frac{(2s-1)^2t}{2s^2(s+1)(s+2)}$

Third day: $\frac{t}{s+2}$ and $\frac{(6s^2-4s+1)t}{6s^3(s+2)}$

(Notice that we need not consider the other expressions, because they are simply additions or subtractions of the expressions listed here, thus forcing them to be whole numbers if those listed here are whole numbers.)

We can agree that some terms in the denominators are factors of t regardless of the value of s.

(a) Neither s nor 2 has a common prime factor with $6s^2 - 4s + 1$, so [third day] $2s^3$ is a factor of t.

(b) $(s+1)$ must be included, since [second day] $s+1$ divides t.

(c) We know [third day] that $(s+2)$ divides t, but it is possible that s and $(s+2)$ have a common factor. If so, the question arises

of whether or not the whole of $(s+2)$ is to be listed as a distinct factor of t. If $(s+2)$ is not to be included as a distinct factor of t, then $s+2$, $2s-1$ [second night], and $6s^2 - 4s + 1$ [third day] must all have a common prime factor, say f. Put $s+2 = fn$, $2s-1 = fm$. Then $2s+4 = 2fn$, and $5 = 2s+4 - (2s-1) = 2fn - fm = f(2n-m)$. Then $f = 5$ (since it was assumed that f was a prime number). Since 5 is the only prime factor possibly shared by $2s-1$ and $s+2$, then 5 must also be a factor of $6s^2 - 4s + 1$ if $s+2$ is not to be included as a distinct factor of t. But this is not possible, which is shown as follows:

Given that 5 is a factor of $s+2$, then 5 is a factor of $(s+2)^2$. Suppose 5 is also a factor of $6s^2 - 4s + 1$. Then 5 is a factor of $(6s^2 - 4s + 1) - (s+2)^2 = 5s^2 - 8s - 3 = 5s^2 - 5s - (3s+3)$, so 5 is a factor of $3(s+1)$, and so 5 is a factor of $s+1$. But this is a contradiction, since $s+1$ and $s+2$ cannot have any common prime factor. Therefore, the supposition must be wrong, and so 5 cannot be a factor of $6s^2 - 4s + 1$. What this whole paragraph implies, of course, is that $s+2$ must be listed as a distinct factor of t.

Now it has been shown that $t = 2s^3(s+1)(s+2)k$, and it can be seen that we can ignore all expressions (listed as First day, First night,…, Third day) except the last one, which can be rewritten as $\frac{(6s^2-4s+1)k}{3}$. It is now easily seen that we have only to ask: Is s divisible by 3? If the answer is yes, then $k = 3$, and $t = 6s^3(s + 1)(s + 2)$. If the answer is no, then $k = 1$ (proof below), and $t = 2s^3(s + 1)(s + 2)$.

[Proof that $k = 1$ if s is not divisible by 3: Since 3 does not divide s, there is an n such that either $s = 3n + 1$ or $s = 3n + 2$. If $s = 3n + 1$, then 3 is a factor of $6s^2 - 4s + 1$. If $s = 3n + 2$, then 3 is a factor of $(s + 1)$. In either case, 3 is a factor of $(6s^2 - 4s + 1)(s + 1)$, and so $k = 1$.]

Summary:
Under the conditions stated in the problem,
$t = 2s^3(s + 1)(s + 2)$ if s is not divisible by 3;
$t = 6s^3(s + 1)(s + 2)$ if s is divisible by 3.

a. 192. $s = 2$, so $t = 2(2^3)(2 + 1)(2 + 2) = 192$

b. 3,240. $s = 3$, so $t = 6(3^3)(3 + 1)(3 + 2) = 3,240$

c. 3,840. $s = 4$, so $t = 2(4^3)(4 + 1)(4 + 2) = 3,840$

d. 10,500. $s = 5$, so $t = 2(5^3)(5 + 1)(5 + 2) = 10,500$

f. a. 193; b. 3,241; c. 3,841; d. 10,501; e, 1 more than the e answer. The altered condition affects only the total gathered each day, since the offending banana was promptly disposed of.

g-h. Not possible. The given conditions are self-contradictory.

g. Put t = the total number of bananas gathered each day. Then each woman got $\frac{t-1}{s}$ the first day.

She discarded 1, leaving, $\frac{t-1-s}{s}$ and ate $\frac{1}{s}$ of those, or $\frac{t-1-s}{s^2}$, leaving $\frac{(s-1)(t-1-s)}{s^2}$. The first night, the newcomer discarded 1, leaving $\frac{(s-1)(t-1-s)-s^2}{s^2}$, and took $\frac{1}{s+1}$ of those, or $\frac{(s-1)(t-1-s)-s^2}{s^2(s+1)}$. At this point, we show as follows that $s = 2$. Referring to the last expression listed, s^2 divides both $(t-1-s)$ [known from the first day] and s^2, so the question is reduced to whether or not $(s + 1)$ divides $(t - 1 - s)(s - 1) - s^2 = (t - 1)(s - 1) - s(s - 1) - s^2 = (t - 1)(s - 1) - (2s^2 - s) = (t - 1)(s - 1) - (2s^2 + 2s - 3s) = (t - 1)(s - 1) - 2s(s + 1) + 3s$. We know that $(s + 1)$ divides $(s + 1)$, and $(s + 1)$ divides $(t - 1)$ [known because of the bananas gathered the second day], so it has to be true that $(s + 1)$ divides $3s$. But s and $(s + 1)$ are mutually prime. Therefore, $(s + 1)$ has to divide 3. But the only positive numbers that divide 3 are 1 and 3. $s \neq 0$, so $s + 1 \neq 1$. Therefore, $s + 1 = 3$, and so $s = 2$.

We can now start again at the first day and use 2 for s.

First day: Each got $\frac{t-1}{s}$; discarded 1, leaving $\frac{t-3}{s}$; ate $\frac{1}{2}$, or $\frac{t-3}{4}$; left $\frac{t-3}{4}$.

First night: From each pile, the newcomer discarded 1, leaving $\frac{t-7}{4}$; took $\frac{1}{3}$ of these, or $\frac{t-7}{12}$; left $\frac{t-7}{6}$.

Second day: Each got $\frac{t-1}{3}$, making a

total of $\frac{t-1}{3} + \frac{t-7}{6} = \frac{t-3}{2}$; discarded 1, leaving $\frac{t-5}{2}$; ate $\frac{1}{4}$ of these, or $\frac{t-5}{8}$.

At this point, we have a contradiction, for it is not possible that 8 divides ($t - 5$) and 4 divides ($t - 3$) [first day].

Proof: Suppose 8 divides ($t - 5$) and 4 divides ($t - 3$).
Put $4k = t - 3$, and put $8n = t - 5$.
Then $4(k - 2n) = t - 3 - (t - 5) = 2$, so $2(k - 2n) = 1$, a contradiction.
Therefore, our supposition must be wrong, so it cannot be true both that 8 divides ($t - 5$) and 4 divides ($t - 3$).

Summary:

It is not possible to have the conditions stated for this problem.

h. First day: Each woman had $\frac{t-1}{s}$ bananas and ate $\frac{1}{s}$ of them, or $\frac{t-1}{s^2}$, leaving $\frac{(s-1)(t-1)}{s^2}$.

First night: From each pile, the newcomer discarded 1, leaving $\frac{(s-1)(t-1) - s^2}{s^2}$, and took $\frac{1}{s+1}$ of them, or $\frac{(s-1)(t-1) - s^2}{s^2(s+1)}$. $\star$

We can foresee a contradiction at this point, proved as follows: s^2 divides ($t - 1$) [first day], and ($s + 1$) divides ($t - 1$) [initial distribution the second day], so $s^2(s + 1)$ has to divide s^2 (from $\star$). But $\frac{s^2}{s^2(s+1)}$ is not a whole number.

Therefore, the conditions stated are not possible.

i. I don't, except for the monkey.

FUN TIME (pp. 98-132)

Not all problems in the booklet are original, but I don't know where to give credit for some of them. Problem **19** was brought to me by a student over twenty years ago. I got ideas for problems **7** and **17c** in one of Dr. Eugene P. Smith's mathematics education classes at Wayne State University, again about twenty years ago. I suspect I first heard some version of problems **12** and **18** in his classes, too. Ideas for some of the other problems came from various books.

(If your students haven't yet discovered recreational mathematics books, they are in for a treat. The Dewey decimal classification number for such books is 793.74, but they can also be found sometimes in the 510 and 513 categories.) Don't be afraid to try out some of the problems (just for fun, of course) on your general math students. They probably won't be able to prove whether or not their answers are right, but they enjoy trying to work out such problems as numbers **1**, **2**, **7**, **10**, **15**, **16**, **18** (give them two numbers to work with in this one), and **19-21**

Encourage your students to do further work on their own. For example, in problem **2**, how much time would the hare have had to spend resting each hour in order to tie the race? Or how much of a head start would the tortoise have to be given in order to win if the hare ran without resting? Or with resting m minutes per hour? What if the length of the course had been more? Less? (How would the answers change?)

Or for problem **16**, does a similar result hold for two-digit numbers? For four-digit numbers? What happens if we add first and then subtract? (Are the results still predictable?)

1. The results of successive steps are shown here. Put r = the result.

    a. n; $n + 7$; $2n + 14$; $2n + 21 = r$;

    $n = \frac{r-21}{2}$

    b. n; $n + 6$; $3n + 18$; $2n + 12 = r$;

    $n = \frac{r-12}{2}$

    c. n; $2n$; $2n - 3$; $10n - 15$; $10n - 11 = r$;

    $n = \frac{r+11}{10}$

    d. n; $n + 6$; $2n + 12$; $2n + 5$; $12n + 30$; $12n + 6$; $4n + 2$; $4n + 44$; $n + 11 = r$; $n = r - 11$

    e. p; $p + y$; $3p + 3y$; $3p + 2y$; $12p + 8y$; $10p + 8y$; $10p + 15y$; $2p + 3y$; $p + 3y = r$; $p = r - 3y$

    f. p; $2p$; $2p + a$; $6p + 3a$; $6p + 3a + y$; $12p + 6a + 2y$; $6p + 2y$; $3p + y = r$;

    $p = \frac{r-y}{2}$

    g. Sure. The variables we used didn't know what kind of numbers they represented, and we never divided by a variable, so no division by zero was involved.

    h. n; n^2; $(n + 1)^2$; $(n + 1)^2 - n^2 = 2n + 1 = r$; $n = \frac{r-1}{2}$

    i. <u>Pat</u>
    Choose: $2n$ **or** $2n + 1$
    Mult: $4n$ **or** $4n + 2$

    <u>Chris</u>
    Choose: $2k + 1$ **or** $2k$

    Mult: $6k + 3$ **or** $6k$

    Add: $2(2n + 3k + 1) + 1$ **or** $2(2n + 1 + 3k)$

    We see that the result is odd or even, according to the kind of number Chris chose.

    j. Yes.
    <u>Pat</u>
    Choose: $2n$ **or** $2n + 1$
    Mult: $2n(2p)$ **or** $(2n + 1)2p$

    <u>Chris</u>
    Choose: $2k + 1$ **or** $2k$
    Mult: $(2k + 1)(2q + 1)$ **or** $2k(2q + 1) = 2(2kq + k + q) + 1$ **or** $2(2kq + k)$

    Add: $2(2pn + 2kq + k + q) + 1$ **or** $2(2np + p + 2kq + k)$

    Again, the result is odd or even, according to the kind of number Chris chose.

    k. Sure. Just switch the names in the proof for **i** above. (Then the result will agree with Pat's choice, rather than Chris's.)

    l. Yes.
    <u>Pat</u>
    Choose: $2n$ **or** $2n + 1$

    <u>Chris</u>
    <u>Choose:</u> $2k + 1$ **or** $2k$

    If g is even, put $g = 2h$. Then the differences will be
    <u>Pat</u>
    $2(n - h)$ **or** $2(n - h) + 1$

    <u>Chris</u>: $2(k - h) + 1$ **or** $2(k - h)$

    Each result has the same parity as the chosen number, so the final answer is not affected.

If g is odd, put $g = 2h + 1$. Then the differences will be

Pat
$2(n - h) - 1$ **or** $2(n - h)$

Chris
$2(k - h)$ **or** $2(k - h) - 1$

This time each result has different parity than the chosen number. Consequently, the parity of the final answer will be the same as the parity of Pat's chosen number.

m- q. The moving of the decimal point is merely a way of multiplying or dividing by 10 (one place) or 100 (two places).

   m. $5n = \frac{n}{2} \times 10$

   n. $\frac{n}{5} = \frac{2n}{10}$

   o. $25n = \frac{n}{4} \times 100$

   p. $\frac{n}{25} = \frac{4n}{100}$

   q. $n = 100q + 00, 25, 50,$ or 75, so the method gives us $4q + 0, 1, 2,$ or 3, which is $\frac{n}{25} = \frac{100q}{25} + \frac{00}{25}, \frac{25}{25}, \frac{50}{25},$ or $\frac{75}{25}$.

 r. (m) Multiply by 10 and divide by 2.

   (n) Multiply by 2 and divide by 10.

   (o) Multiply by 100 and divide by 4.

   (p) Multiply by 4 and divide by 100.

 s. $(10t + u)[10t + (10 - u)] =$
$100t^2 + 10t(10 - u + u) + u(10 - u) =$
$100t(t + 1) + u(10 - u)$

t. $(10t + u)[10(10 - t) + u] =$
$100t(10 - t) + 10u(t + 10 - t) + u^2 =$
$100t(10 - t) + 100u + u^2 =$
$100[t(10 - t) + u] + u^2$

u. If the number has only one or two digits, then the test is self-evident. Otherwise, the number can be expressed as $100n + 10t + u$, where n can be any positive integer. Since 4 divides $100n$, the only question is whether or not 4 divides $10t + u$, and that is what the test states.

v. The proof is the same as for **u**, except that the number is expressed as $1000n + 100h + 10t + u$. 8 divides $1000n$, so the question is whether or not it divides the last three digits, $100h + 10t + u$.

2. $t = \frac{D}{r}$. The tortoise's time was $\frac{5}{\frac{1}{4}} =$ 20 hours, so he finished at 20 hours past noon, or 8:00 the next morning. The hare traveled at 10 mph for $\frac{10}{60}$ of each hour, making his average rate $\frac{1}{6}$ of 10, or $1\frac{2}{3}$ mph. Then his time was $\frac{5}{1\frac{2}{3}} = 3$ hours. He started off 15 hours after noon, or at 3:00 the next morning, so he finished at 6:00 that morning (two hours before the tortoise finished).

Moral:
(1) Don't assume that all stories about tortoises and hares must end as Aesop's fable did.

(2) The underdog doesn't always win.

(3) Even when one tries to be fair, s(he) may not succeed.

(4) Some people just aren't cut out for racing.

(5) The race may not always be to the swiftest, but it sure does seem to be most of the time.

(6) Some people are natural winners in certain kinds of competitions.

(7) The slow but steady plodder does not necessarily do the job better than the one who works sporadically.

(8) etc.

3. **A.** Successive steps are: n; n^2; $n + 1$; $(n + 1)^2$; $2n^2 + 2n + 1$; $2n^2 + 2n$; $n^2 + n = n(n + 1)$

   B. Successive steps are: n; n^2; $n + 2$; $(n + 2)^2$; $4n + 4$; $n + 1$

4. $x = y$, so the division in the fifth line was division by 0.

5. $y + g = s$, so $g = s - y$. Now $y < g$, so $y < s - y$, and so $y < \frac{s}{2}$. Then $y - \frac{s}{2}$ is negative. Therefore, the square root of $(y - \frac{s}{2})^2$ is $\frac{s}{2} - y$, not $y - \frac{s}{2}$.

   Thus, the fallacy is in the next to last line of the proof.

6. **a.** Successive steps are: n; $3n$; $3n + 15$; $12n + 60$; $10n + 60$; $50n + 300$; $60n + 300$; $10n + 50$; $7n + 50$; $7n + 63$; $n + 9$; n.

   b. Yes. There was no division by the chosen number.

   c-d. Sure. The n in part **a** didn't know it was a whole number.

7. Answers for magic squares are given by rows (1st, 2nd, 3rd).

   a. 4, 9, 2; 3, 5, 7; 8, 1, 6

   (1) 45; 3; 15

(2) Suggest they proceed in an orderly way—i.e., hold one number constant while they see how many ways the rest of the sum can be made. They will come out with more combinations than the eight needed for the square, but the extras will be duplications. The method suggested will answer part (3) for us.

with 1: 9 and 5, 8 and 6

with 2: 9 and 4, 8 and 5, 7 and 6

with 3: 8 and 4, 7 and 5

with 4: 9 and 2, 8 and 3, 6 and 5

with 5: 9 and 1, 8 and 2, 7 and 3, 6 and 4

with 6: 8 and 1, 7 and 2, 5 and 4

with 7: 6 and 2, 5 and 3

with 8: 6 and 1, 5 and 2, 4 and 3

with 9: 5 and 1, 4 and 2

(3) Refer to the list above. First, the center number (*e* in the given diagram) must be used four times, and 5 is the only number that qualifies, so 5 goes in the center.

Second, the corner numbers are used three times each, so this forces 2, 4, 6, and 8 to be in the corners. Choose any one of these and place it in any corner. One of the remaining three numbers will be forced into the opposite corner. The two remaining numbers can be placed in either corner, for one placement is simply a reflection (across a diagonal) of the other. Similarly, if a different corner had been chosen to start with, the resulting square would be a rotation or a reflection of the square we have.

Third, we now have the center and the four corners filled, so all other positions are forced.

b-c. Yes. We simply add 1 (for part **b**) or 2 (for part **c**) to each number in the square we've already made.

d-i. Yes. Any arithmetic sequence of nine numbers can be used. To make the square wanted, we refer to the square we already have. We put the first number of the sequence where our 1 is, the second number where our 2 is, and so on. (That's if we want to do it the easy way. Otherwise, we can always go through a proof for each case, or we can use trial and error.)

j. No. They don't have to be an arithmetic sequence, but there are other requirements to be fulfilled, among which are (1) the sum must be divisible by 9; (2) the sum divided by 9, call it n, must be one of the nine numbers (it goes in the center); (3) the other eight numbers must form conjugate pairs with n—i.e., if $n + d$ is one of the numbers, then $n - d$ must also be one of the numbers.

Letting n be the center number, and letting $n + d$ and $n + e$ be in the upper left and right corners, all numbers of the magic square are determined, and the square is:

$n + d, n - (d + e), n + e; n - d + e, n,$

$n + d - e; n - e, n + d + e, n - d.$

k-n. Yes. There are no particular problems here. For a simple proof, choose nine consecutive numbers to include the kinds being questioned, and fill in the square as we did for items **b** through **i**.

o-p. Yes. A simple way to make such a square is to use what we found in part **i**: choose a number (decimal for part **o**, fraction for part **p**) to be n and then place $1n, 2n,...,9n$ in the square in the usual way. (Although the n in part **i** was a whole number, it doesn't have to be.)

q. No. Given that the four numbers are arranged

$$a \quad b$$
$$c \quad d,$$

then $a + b = a + d = a + c$, so $b = d = c$.

Similarly, $a = b = c$, so $a = b = c = d$, and we said the questions would refer to nontrivial magic squares.

r. Yes. 6, 4, 72; 144, 12, 1; 2, 36, 24 is one such square. (When the students have determined that the answer is "yes," ask if such a square could contain fractions.)

8. The last step divides by zero.

9. The second step is wrong. We are given b < a, so b - a < 0, and when an inequality is multiplied by a negative number, the order of the inequality changes. So the correct second step would be $b(b - a) > a(b - a)$. Following through to the last step, the result is $(b - a)^2 > 0$, which is true.

10. When the students have proved their answers to these problems, ask them what happens if the restrictions are changed. This is an open-ended question, and some of the better students might be able to find a general formula to account for any restriction.

a.

Choose:	h	m	s
Regroup:	$h - 1$	$m + 60 - 1$	$s + 60$
Reverse:	s	m	h
Subtract:	$h - 1 - s$	59	$s + 60 - h$
Reverse:	$s + 60 - h$	59	$h - 1 - s$
Add:	59	118	59
Regroup:	60	58	59

b.

Choose:	b	p	q
Regroup:	$b - 1$	$p + 4 - 1$	$q + 8$
Reverse:	q	p	b
Subtract:	$b - 1 - q$	3	$q + 8 - b$
Reverse:	$q + 8 - b$	3	$b - 1 - q$
Add:	7	6	7
Regroup:	8	2	7

c.

Choose:	p	z	d
Regroup:	$p - 1$	$z + 16 - 1$	$d + 16$
Reverse:	d	z	p
Subtract:	$p - 1 - d$	15	$d + 16 - p$
Reverse:	$d + 16 - p$	15	$p - 1 - d$
Add:	15	30	15
Regroup:	16	14	15

d.

Choose:	p	z	d
Regroup:	$p - 1$	$z + 12 - 1$	$d + 8$
Reverse:	d	z	p
Subtract:	$p - 1 - d$	11	$d + 8 - p$
Reverse:	$d + 8 - p$	11	$p - 1 - d$
Add:	7	22	7
Regroup:	8	10	7

e.

Choose:	y	w	d
Regroup:	$y - 1$	$w + 52 - 1$	$d + 7$
Reverse:	d	w	y
Subtract:	$y - 1 - d$	51	$d + 7 - y$
Reverse:	$d + 7 - y$	51	$y - 1 - d$
Add:	6	102	6
Regroup:	7	50	6

f.

Choose:	y	f	i
Regroup:	$y - 1$	$f + 3 - 1$	$i + 12$
Reverse:	i	f	y

Subtract:	$y - 1 - i$	2	$i + 12 - y$
Reverse:	$i + 12 - y$	2	$y - 1 - i$
Add:	11	4	11
Regroup:	12	1	11

11. (1) m

(2) $4m$

(3) $4m + 7$

(4) $20m + 35$

(5) $20m + 15$

(6) $100m + 75$

(7) $100m + 81$

(8) $200m + 162$

(9) $200m + 2d + 162$

(10) $200m + 2d + 100$

(11) $1{,}000m + 10d + 500$

(12) $1{,}000m + 10d + 535$

(13) $6{,}000m + 60d + 3{,}210$

(14) $6{,}000m + 60d + 1{,}110$

(15) $2{,}000m + 20d + 370$

(16) $10{,}000m + 100d + 1{,}850$

(17) $10{,}000m + 100d + y + 1{,}850$

(18) $10{,}000m + 100d + y$

12. The problem here is simply to find the sum of the infinite series $1 + \frac{1}{2} + \frac{1}{2^2} + \frac{1}{2^3} + \ldots$. Using the standard formula, the sum is $\frac{1}{1 - \frac{1}{2}} = \frac{1}{\frac{1}{2}}$ = 2 minutes.

13. The third step is in error. The rule given holds only for positive b. (The rule really states, "For $b > 0, \ldots$")

14. The next-to-last step is in error: The rule given holds only when the numerators are nonzero. (Putting $x = 4$ in the initial equation will show the equation to be $0 = 0$. And, of course, $x = 4$ makes $5x - 20 = 0$. The rule really states, "If two equal fractions have equal nonzero numerators, then ....")

15. Write the number chosen as $100h + 10t + u$. Then the tacking-on process makes the number $100,000h + 10,000t + 1,000u + 100h + 10t + u = 100,100h + 10,010t + 1,001u = 1,001(100h + 10t + u)$. But $1,001 = 7(11)(13)$, so when $1,001(100h + 10t + u)$ is divided successively by 7, 11, and 13, it is in fact being divided by 1,001, leaving $100h + 10t + u$, the chosen number.

16. (1) $100h + 10t + u$

(2) $100u + 10t + h$

It is assumed that $h > u$. If not, then switch the h and the u in the steps that follow:

(3) Since $h > u$, we will have to regroup before we can subtract, just as we did for problem **10**. Then the problem will be

$100(h - 1) + 10(t + 10 - 1) + (u + 10)$

$100u \qquad + 10t \qquad\qquad + h$

Subtract:
$100(h - 1 - u) + 10(9) + (u + 10 - h)$

(4) $100(u + 10 - h) + 10(9) + (h - 1 - u)$

(5) $100(9) + 10(18) + 9 = 900 + 180 + 9 = 1089$

17. a. Suppose a and b are both odd numbers. Put $a = 2k + 1$, $b = 2m + 1$. Then $c^2 = a^2 + b^2 = 2(2k^2 + 2k + 2m^2 + 2m + 1)$. Put the parenthesized expression $= n$. Then $c^2 = 2n$, where n is odd. Then 2 is a factor of c^2, and so 2 is a factor of c. But if 2 is a factor of c, then 4 is a factor of $c^2 = 2n$, which implies 2 is a factor of n. But this is not possible, because n is odd. Therefore, the supposition must be wrong, and so at least one of a and b has to be an even number.

b. Keep in mind that a, b, and c are all assumed to be integral. If the legs were the same length, we'd have $2a^2 = c^2$, so $a\sqrt{2} = c$, which would mean that c was not integral, a contradiction. Therefore, the legs can't be the same length.

c. (1) a, b
(2) a^2, b^2
(3) $2ab$
(4) $a^2 - b^2$ (**or** $b^2 - a^2$)
(5) $a^2 + b^2$

It works because $(3)^2 + (4)^2 = (5)^2$. (Is that some kind of pun?) In other words, $(2ab)^2 + (a^2 - b^2)^2 = 4a^2b^2 + a^4 - 2a^2b^2 + b^4 = a^4 + 2a^2b^2 + b^4 = (a^2 + b^2)^2$, thus satisfying the converse of the Pythagorean Theorem. [The converse of this theorem is also true, of course. If your students haven't already seen a proof (of the converse), ask them how it could be proved.]

18. The first thing to realize is that it takes a chicken $1\frac{1}{2}$ days, not 1 day, to lay an egg.

This is more easily seen if we approach it from another angle. Suppose you and two other people all work at the same rate, and it takes you three days to do a certain job if you work alone. Now if there are three of those jobs to be done, and if all three of you work on them, one person to each job, then three people will do three jobs in three days. And it took three days, not one day, for each person to do one job. As a general rule, we have number of jobs you do =

$$\frac{\text{number of days you work}}{\text{number of days you need to do one job}}.$$

Having established that, we see that if one chicken works for d days, that chicken will lay $\frac{d}{1\frac{1}{2}}$ eggs. And if

c chickens work for d days, they will lay $\frac{cd}{1\frac{1}{2}}$ eggs. So, putting e = the

number of eggs laid, we have the general equation $e = \frac{2}{3}(cd)$.

Now that the hard work is done, we easily find the answers to the problems:

a. $e = \frac{2}{3}(9)(10) = 60$

b. $e = \frac{2}{3}(c)(12) = 8c$

c. $e = \frac{2}{3}(12)(d) = 8d$

d. Solving the equation above, we have $d = \frac{3e}{2c} = \frac{3(12)}{2c} = \frac{18}{c}$.

e. $d = \frac{3e}{2c} = \frac{3e}{2(12)} = \frac{e}{8}$

f. Solving the equation above, we

have $c = \frac{3e}{2d} = \frac{3e}{2(12)} = \frac{e}{8}$.

g. $c = \frac{3e}{2d} = \frac{3(12)}{2d} = \frac{18}{d}$.

3 must be a factor of either c or d, and 2 must be a factor of e.

19. In order to decipher the next-to-last paragraph, it is helpful to break it into four parts:

(a) The monkey's mother is half as old as the monkey will be

(b) when the monkey is three times as old as its mother was

(c) when the mother was half as old as the monkey will be

(d) when the monkey is twice as old as it is now.

Put A = the age (in years) of the mother now.
Put a = the age (in years) of the monkey now.

Then (d) is $2a$, and (c) is $\frac{1}{2}$ of $2a$, or a. This makes (b) $3a$, which makes (a) $A = \frac{1}{2}$ of $3a$, or $\frac{3a}{2}$.

From the third paragraph, $A + a = 30$, so $a = 12$, $A = 18$.

Continuing with the third paragraph, we have

age of monkey = 12 years
age of mother = 18 years
length of rope = 12 feet
weight of monkey = 18 ounces

Combining this with the first and second paragraphs, we have

weight of rope = 4 pounds = 64 ounces
weight of weight = 18 ounces

The fourth paragraph will then give

us weight of banana + 9 ounces = $\frac{1}{4}$ (18 + 64) ounces, so weight of

banana = $\frac{23}{2}$ ounces. Then from the

third paragraph, the length of the

banana is $\frac{\frac{23}{2}}{2}$ inches = $\frac{23}{4}$ inches = $5\frac{3}{4}$ inches.

20. There is the same amount of vanilla in the almond bottle as there is almond in the vanilla bottle.

Put t = the number of teaspoonsful of flavoring in each bottle at the beginning.

When the cook puts the almond in the vanilla bottle, the vanilla bottle contains (t + 1) teaspoonsful, of which t is vanilla and 1 is almond. The bottle is shaken, mixing the contents, so every teaspoonful is now $\frac{1}{t+1}$ of almond and $\frac{1}{t+1}$ of vanilla.

In the meantime, the almond bottle contains (t - 1) teaspoonsful of almond. When the teaspoonful of mixture is added, the almond bottle contains t teaspoonsful again, of which $\frac{1}{t+1}$ teaspoonful is vanilla.

The vanilla bottle contains (after the second transfer) t teaspoonsful of mixture, and since every teaspoonful is $\frac{1}{t+1}$ of almond, there are $\frac{1}{t+1}$ teaspoonsful of almond.

21. Distance is a continuous function (of rate and time), but the argument states that the total distance to be traveled is the sum of the infinite series $\frac{1}{2} + \frac{1}{2^2} + \frac{1}{2^3} + ...$, claiming that

the total can never be reached

because there is no last term in the series. In other words, the argument treats distance as a finite series of discrete intervals, thereby ignoring its continuity. It is similar to saying that a segment cannot have an infinite number of points because it is made up of discrete points.

22. $S = 2(\frac{1}{3})(K + 10)$

$\frac{5}{3}D = S + K - 10$

$J + 2 = \frac{1}{4}(S + K + D + J)$

$S + J = D + K$

So Donna is 15, Juan is 14, Karen is 17, and Serge is 18.

23. $b + c = 100$

$2b + 4c = 260$ **or** $2b + 4c = 270$, but this second equation forces the number of horses to be a nonwhole number, thus showing that the figure of 270 is wrong.

$2b + 4c + 4h = 300$
$4c + 4h + 4d = 200$

So there were 70 birds, 30 cows, 10 dogs, and 10 horses. (Karla knew because she was good at figuring out systems of equations in her head.)

24. Of each statement made, half is true and half is false. The statements are relisted here, using (a) and (b) as the two halves of each statement. Notice that the paraphrasing does not affect the truth values of the statements within the context of the problem.

1(a) $comp = $quad + $500

1(b) Jim can run faster than Kate.

2(a) There is no quad system.

2(b) 1(b) is false.

3(a) $(quad + comp) = $(car + cycle) - $900

3(b) $cycle = $(\frac{1}{2}$)$car

4(a) $cycle = $(\frac{2}{3}$)$car

4(b) $comp > $(car + cycle)

5(a) 4(b) is true.

5(b) Jim can run faster than Debbie.

6(a) 5(b) is false and 1(b) is false.

6(b) There is no computer system.

7(a) 6(b) is false and the system was purchased last week.

7(b) 1(b) is true.

8(a) 6(b) is false and the system was purchased two weeks ago.

8(b) 1(a) is false.

Now, keeping in mind that the truth values of (a) and (b) for a given number must be opposites, we will see if we can force a contradiction. We will start by supposing that 1(b) is false.

true	false	Reason for decision
	1(b)	Supposition.
1(a)		1(b) is false.
	7(b)	1(b) is false.
7(a)		7(b) is false.

true	false	Reason for decision
	8(a)	7(a) is true.
8(b)		8(a) is false.

But this is a contradiction, since 1(a) and 8(b) cannot both be true. Therefore, the supposition that 1(b) is false has to be wrong, and so 1(b) is true. We start again, in order to verify that all statements are consistent.

true	false	Reason for decision
1(b)		Forced by previous contradiction.
	1(a)	1(b) is true.
	2(b)	1(b) is true.
2(a)		2(b) is false.
7(b)		1(b) is true.
	7(a)	7(b) is true.
8(b)		1(a) is false.
	8(a)	8(b) is true.
	6(a)	1(b) is true.
6(b)		6(a) is false.
	4(b)	6(b) is true.
4(a)		4(b) is false.
	3(b)	4(a) is true.
3(a)		3(b) is false.
	5(a)	4(b) is false.
5(b)		5(a) is false.

There are no contradictions here, and so the problem can be solved. Since 2(a), 3(a), 6(b), and 4(a) are all true, 3(a) and 4(a) can be rewritten as

$$car + cycle = 900$$
$$cycle = \tfrac{2}{3} \ car.$$

So the car's cost was $540, and the motorcycle's cost was $360. (The costs of the computer system and the quad system were, of course, $0.) Then 1(b) and 5(b) imply that Jim can run faster than both Debbie and Kate.

25. The formula needed is $A = P(1 + r)^n$.

a. $P = \dfrac{A}{1.01^{32}} = \dfrac{\$4,124.82}{1.01^{32}} = \$3,000$

b. $A = \dfrac{\$3,000}{1.06^{32}} = \$19,360.16$

c. $A = \dfrac{\$3,000}{1.09^{32}} = \$47,289.99$

d. $A = \dfrac{\$3,000}{1.12^{32}} = \$112,745.18$

26. (a) $100h + 10t + u$. This will have to be regrouped for the subtraction in part (c) below, so we will have $100(h - 1) + 10(t + 10 - 1) + (u + 10)$.

(b) $100u + 10t + h$

(c) [If $u > h$, regroup (b) instead of (a), and subtract (a) from (b).] $100(h - 1 - u) + 10(6) + (u + 10 - h)$

(d) $100(u + 10 - h) + 10(6) + (h - 1 - u)$

(e) $100(6) + 10(15) + 6 = 100(6 + 1) + 10(15 - 10) + 6 = 1000 + 10(5) + 6 = 1,056$
(Notice that this answer is analogous to the base ten answer for problem **16**, 1089, since 5 = 7 - 2 and 6 = 7 - 1, just as 8 = 10 - 2 and 9 = 10 - 1.) 1,056 in base seven = in base ten $1(7^3) + 5(7) + 6 = 343 + 35 + 6 = 384$.

27. This is a tough one for high school students. While both the given series and the series immediately following it are convergent, all series following "Put S =" are divergent and therefore have infinite sums, and we cannot use finite arithmetic methods to take sums or differences of infinite numbers. Consequently, the fallacy in the proof starts at "Then S =" and continues from there to the end.